BARE ESSENTIALS

CYAN|CAMPUS

BARE ESSENTIALS

THE ALDI WAY TO RETAIL SUCCESS

DIETER BRANDES

Translated by William Hadfield-Burkardt

Copyright © 2005 Campus Verlag GmbH, Frankfurt/Main

First published in German as *Konsequent einfach: Die ALDI Erfolgs-story* by Campus Verlag, Frankfurt/Main, 1998

This English translation first published in Great Britain in 2004 by Cyan/Campus Books, an imprint of

Cyan Communications Limited
4.3 The Ziggurat
60–66 Saffron Hill
London EC1N 8QX
www.cyanbooks.com

Reprinted 2005

A CIP record for this book is available from the British Library

ISBN 0-9542829-7-3

Printed and bound in Great Britain by
TJ International, Padstow, Cornwall

"What is essential is invisible to the eye."
The Little Prince, Antoine de Saint-Exupéry

CONTENTS

NOTE ON THE ENGLISH EDITION

Like many translations, this book is being published a few years after the original edition. Since it first appeared in Germany in 1998, where it featured in the list of non-fiction bestsellers for over a year, the world of ALDI has inevitably moved on. The biggest change is that ALDI has expanded its offering to include many more non-food items: computers, footwear, household appliances, gardening implements and so on. These goods already account for 20 to 25 percent of total sales.

The other key development is that ALDI is still enjoying strong growth in both its sales and its profits. Up to 85 percent of all German families shop at almost 4,000 stores across the country. In 2004, ALDI's worldwide sales are expected to exceed 40 billion euros, with profits before tax of 1.5 billion euros.

Despite the passage of time, though, the message of this book still holds true. It is not just about ALDI, but about a management philosophy based on simplicity that has universal relevance and value. As many companies know to their cost, it is all too easy to get sidetracked into providing ever more performance projections, management reports and market analyses and to lose sight of what really matters – the bare essentials.

This is why so many businesses both within and beyond the retail sector want to understand what ALDI is doing and how it manages to conquer complexity. This English edition will make ALDI's tremendous success story accessible to readers across the English-speaking world for the first time.

PREFACE

Soon after I left ALDI, an editor from the leading German news weekly *Der Spiegel* called me and asked if I would be open to the idea of writing about the company. True to the ALDI custom of discretion, I turned him down.

Uncompromising opposition to publicity exemplifies ALDI's asceticism. It is something I have always supported, and I still think it right for the vast majority of companies today. Most corporate statements and executive interviews do little but pander to the vanity of the CEO or the managers. In many cases, too, they are used to prepare the way for the sale of a company, showcasing only its good points. The information they provide is useful only to the competition. It does nothing for the customer – when the customer, surely, is what it's all about.

Now that the ALDI concept is more than 50 years old and both the company's founders, Karl and Theo Albrecht, are over the age of 80, I feel the time has come to write about the "ALDI phenomenon"; I can do so from a distance, after a number of years spent at other companies, and with an eye for the business essentials. Remarkable though it may seem, a book about the ALDI "miracle" has never before appeared in the book shops – although many economists and journalists have written about it again and again.

ALDI, controlled by family trusts and consisting of a group of smallish companies with no need to publish detailed accounts, has always been able to remain something of a financial mystery. In addition, the principle of confidentiality and the loyalty of employees have historically helped to prevent the whole picture from being publicized. In recent years, however, a few employees have switched to competitors and have, presumably, taken their "figures" with them – even though, as at every other company, this is prohibited. It can be assumed that this is how more and more accurate figures from ALDI have found their way into business publications and cleared up some of the uncertainty surrounding the organization's standing: the public is no longer solely dependent on estimates. And yet, to paraphrase industry specialist Hans Otto Eglau,[1] who has been following ALDI since its foundation, the company's figures remain, in principle, more closely guarded than secret service codes.

Astrid Paprotta and Regina Schneider, whose best-selling cookbook *ALDIdente*[2] was written as a tribute to the discounter and virtually gave it cult status, call ALDI "a strange empire." Everyone is familiar with it, but hardly anybody talks about it. Perhaps because it is an empire built on self-evident principles.

The purpose of this book is not to supply the reader with the very latest official statistics in a quantitative study of ALDI. Such a study would, in my opinion, be peripheral. People repeatedly ask questions about turnover, the break-even point or the net margin – but what is so interesting about isolated figures? Isn't understanding the inner workings of this successful company more important? Quantitative data can form only a limited basis for comparing companies and is not very helpful. It should be much more important for competitors to think about the purpose and goals of their own businesses.

What determines success is primarily the collection of values known as the corporate culture. I will focus on this, on organization and leadership, and on the vital business principles. My account will make clear that nearly everything really is as simple and straightforward as it seems.

I consider it entirely possible to export the principles and practices that work for ALDI to many other companies in many other sectors. Entrepreneurs who have recognized that they can put quite a few aspects of ALDI's practices to use are reaping the benefits.

Roller, for example, Germany's largest furniture chain store, is happy to refer to itself as the "ALDI of the furniture industry." The company commits itself to being the price leader at every one of its locations. Founder Hans-Joachim Tessner came up with the idea of creating a furniture discount outlet following the example of the Albrecht brothers in 1969.[3] Similarly, Thomas Hofmann, the managing partner of the sweet makers Hofmann GmbH & Co. KG, once described his company in an interview as "the ALDI of the sweets and chocolates business."[4] He respected ALDI's success and made close adherence to its methods a business management rule.

This examination of ALDI's characteristics and principles will also make clear where critical errors are made in retailing. This is something I did not realize until I left: my years at ALDI made my ability to scrutinize others more acute.

My experiences outside of Germany highlighted ALDI's special qualities to me. The most important involved setting up a discount chain modeled on ALDI in Turkey. Involvement in the expansion of the ALDI companies in the Netherlands, Belgium and Denmark and in the purchase and management of affiliations in the US was also very illuminating. My experiences in other German companies were very different, however.

Seeing what went on there compels me to point out how much better they could do by following ALDI's example.

My conclusions are based largely on insights I gained as a general manager and member of the administrative board[5] at ALDI North, and from talking to the people there over the past few years.[6]

In recent years, some aspects of ALDI's corporate culture have changed – and not, in my judgment, for the better. In this book I present what ALDI has done successfully – the principles and methods of business management that are most suitable for today and tomorrow.

When I showed some excerpts from this book to Monika Linde, who as an outstanding professional coach is especially sensitive to underlying themes, her response was that this would become a book on ethics. At first I was somewhat baffled and I reviewed what I had written. But her assessment is absolutely right. Ethics have a role in business, and ALDI is, in many respects, an ethics-based business, proving that it is perfectly possible to make a lot of money while retaining scruples. There is nothing unethical about earning money or money *per se*. The ancient Romans used to say: *"pecunia non olet"* (money does not stink).

This book is unquestionably a book with an ethical dimension and a "cultural book" – the contribution ALDI's corporate culture has made to its success should not be underestimated. My account of ALDI will bring back memories of the old values; crucially, it will show that these values can generate profits. People will see the significance and the benefits of ethical and moral behavior in addition to the efficiency of a "technically proficient," contemporary business.

ALDI was the best school in corporate leadership for me. And I am grateful. And if the dates contained in Karl Albrecht's 1953 lecture are correct, this book should also be by way of a homage, a late commemoration of the company's 50th anniversary. I know, though, that the Albrecht brothers, with their distaste for publicity, will not welcome it unreservedly.

I would like to thank the former administrative board member, Otto Hübner. Despite a number of differences of opinion over the years, I have always appreciated his loyalty to principles. Aptly referred to in *manager magazin* as Theo Albrecht's right-hand man, he has consistently kept the ALDI faith. He recruited me as "promising talent" from co-op in Kiel and assigned me to ALDI North in Herten, Westphalia in 1971. Later, he appointed me as general manager in Nortorf, a small town of 6,000 in Schleswig-Holstein that was later to become the site of the Albrecht

Foundation. In 1975 I was finally made the third member of the administrative board in Essen alongside Hübner and Theo Albrecht.

I would also like to thank Aziz G. Zapsu who unwittingly promoted this project by being eager to understand both ALDI and the principle of simplicity. In a mere five years he opened 600 discount stores in Turkey. Aziz and his brother Cüneyd have already been called the "Albrecht brothers of Turkey" by the German business weekly *Wirtschaftswoche*.

This book is meant to be consistent with the fundamental ALDI principles. I hope it is easy to understand. I have tried to avoid management speak and buzzwords that sound clever but mean little and to spare the reader unnecessary filler. I wanted to describe the essentials: the essentials in the context of an operating business.

I would like to thank Campus for its support – in particular, for the many helpful suggestions made by Karin Beiküfner, Britta Kroker and the late Frank Schwoerer.

Today, ALDI has businesses in 10 European countries, in the United States and Australia. Large companies in traditional industries and in the IT industry (such as IBM, Hewlett-Packard, SAP), banks (Credit Suisse), retailers (OBI, OTTO Versand, AVA) and industrial manufacturers like BASF and mid-sized companies are equally interested in its story. They all want to learn from ALDI. In 300 presentations and seminars to date in Germany, Austria, Switzerland, the Netherlands, Italy, Ireland, the UK and Turkey, I have been able to show entrepreneurs how ALDI manages its operations according to the principle of simplicity.

The Albrecht brothers are now considered the richest men in Europe. According to the *Forbes* World's Richest People list, their assets have ranked them third in 2002, 2003 *and* 2004. They are, therefore, interesting to many people.

Chinese speakers in Taiwan are already able to read in a Chinese edition of *Bare Essentials* what has contributed to ALDI's success. And this English language edition will give many other companies in the world an opportunity to learn how the ALDI brand of management works. The ALDI system is not exclusively a retail discount system, but a management and organization system that can be applied in any business.

Originally, the word discount meant a price cut in exchange for lower quality. Today, we can understand discount as an offer without certain incidentals. At ALDI, there is no wide range of products – we only stock the 700 most important items bought to meet daily consumer needs.

Similarly, Southwest Airlines in the United States offers low-cost travel with absolutely no frills.

This edition is an updated version of the German language original and contains an additional section that compares ALDI with Wal-Mart and Jack Welch's General Electric. Wal-Mart has entered the European market and is coming up against ALDI in Germany and England. GE is interesting because Jack Welch worked on principles that are similar to ALDI's. In the German edition, I argued that ALDI had more in common with Toyota than its German competitor, Tengelmann/A&P. Having learned more about GE, I can say that ALDI, Toyota and GE have formed a three-star constellation of simplicity, concentration, efficiency and persistence.

I would also like to thank William Hadfield-Burkardt for his proficient completion of a demanding translation.

Dieter Brandes

Shared strengths:
What ALDI has in common with
Wal-Mart and General Electric

One way to understand ALDI's success is to compare it with two of its peers, both leaders in their industries.

The world's top retailers

In 1998, Wal-Mart launched itself into the German market by taking over the 70 retail outlets of the Wertkauf Group. German retail managers held a conference to discuss what they could expect and whether Wal-Mart might pose a threat. When I addressed the conference, I argued that we should take Wal-Mart very seriously, not because it is so big, but because it is so much like ALDI. Wal-Mart's founder Sam Walton once said: "Most of the values and the rules and the techniques we've relied on have stayed the same the whole way. Some of them are such simple common-sense old favorites that they hardly seem worth mentioning."

That is exactly how Karl and Theo Albrecht would have talked about their principles and techniques. Sam Walton's precepts implicitly guide ALDI too. Sam was as obsessed with detail as the Albrecht brothers. He emphasized item merchandising, and "really loved to pick an item – maybe the most basic merchandise – and then call attention on it." ALDI might well have concurred with the philosophy he expressed in his book: "For my whole career in retail, I have stuck by one guiding principle. It's a simple one, and I have repeated it over and over in this book until I'm sure you're sick to death of it. But I'm going to say it again and again anyway: the secret of successful retailing is to give the customer what they want." (*Sam Walton: Made in America – My Story*, by Sam Walton with John Huey, Bantam Books, 1993.)

This is the crux of it all: the needs of customers in different types of supermarket differ. A Wal-Mart customer wants to find everything under one roof at low prices; an ALDI customer is looking for something else. ALDI has no reason to fear Wal-Mart, because ALDI is pursuing a different corporate concept. Consider these numbers:

ALDI sells	700 items
WAL-Mart sells	100,000 items
ALDI turnover	US $44 billion
WAL-MART turnover	US $300 billion
which translate into:	
ALDI turnover per item	US $63 million
WAL-MART turnover per item	US $3 million

These ratios result in completely different strategies, organizations and cost structures. Even so, both companies are extremely successful. Just how successful can be measured by the yardsticks of growth and profitability. Wal-Mart and ALDI have been the most successful retailers in the world for over 50 years. Both were founded in the post-war period, have operated using similar methods and have achieved similar levels of success. I look at ALDI's rules in this book; Sam Walton's "10 rules for building a business" are documented in *Sam Walton: Made in America – My Story*.

At Wal-Mart they say: "We are different"; ALDI says much the same. Sam Walton declared "We think small" and referred to his "simplicity concept"; simplicity is also one of ALDI's guiding principles. Wal-Mart makes a habit of trying things out to see if they work; trial and error is the ALDI way too. Sam Walton and his managers knew that there is no magic formula for success, but that numerous small things contribute to it, a conviction that ALDI shares. Retail is detail: paying attention to all the success factors over decades. That is the art, and that is no secret.

Wal-Mart, like ALDI, has retained its original convictions despite rapid growth over many years. One of them is the principle of delegation: "The bigger Wal-Mart gets, the more essential it is that we think small. Because that's exactly how we have become a huge corporation – by not acting like one. And I suspect thinking small is an approach that almost any business could profit from. A lot of bureaucracy is really the product of some empire builder's ego."

Succeeding by being different

ALDI and General Electric differ in their structures and in their business lines: one sells tins of beans and bottles of detergent, the other power plants and aircraft engines. Yet the companies are guided by the same business principles. Each is so different from its industry competitors that it is fair to say that its success derives from being different

This book will explore ALDI's idiosyncrasies: its corporate culture, philosophy, working principles and organizational methods. It will show that difference is what makes for success in the long run. Everyone knows that the most successful manager in the world, Jack Welch, turned GE into the world's most valuable company by managing in a different way from anyone else. He put forward the following principles, and implemented them in his company with discipline and rigor:

"Too often people are too complicated. Everyone wants to put all the data that they can think of on a page. My idea is, simplify it. Enrich the language; that carries the day, not the paper. There's no trade-off in terms of the information content, not for me, because I can't do anything with all the information. It doesn't help most people at the next level to have all that data. What they need to know is: What are the strategic questions I have to answer? What are the variables?"(From Jack Welch and the GE Way: Management insights and leadership secrets of the legendary CEO, *by Robert Slater, McGraw-Hill Education, 1998.)*

"People always overestimate how complex business is. This isn't rocket science."

"For the next couple of years, we'll be focusing very hard on simplifying: on getting simpler with communications with each other, with presentations, with products. We'll concentrate on products that have fewer parts and simple designs. Business tends to overcomplicate things – most of life tends to over-complicate things."

"Create a clear, simple, reality-based vision . . . and communicate it to all constituencies."

"Don't focus on the numbers. Numbers aren't the vision; numbers aren't the product. I never talk about numbers."

"People waste a lot of time on making budgets. They waste energy. We can't afford to waste time. Budgets enervate. Stretch targets energize."

"Run the company like a family grocery store."

"You've got to balance freedom with some control."

"Redefine the traditional concept of management. Listen to the people. Give them the right and responsibility to come up with their own ideas for solving problems."

"If you have a simple, consistent message, and you keep on repeating it, eventually that's what happens. Simplicity, consistency and repetition – that's how you get through. Be simple, be consistent and hammer your massage home. The only way to change people's minds is with consistency."

ALDI would probably echo all these sentiments, as would Wal-Mart. They show that basic principles of healthy common sense and business sense are the makings of success, not knowledge management, budgets and data warehouses.

Introduction
ALDI: A portrait in miniature

"Our only consideration in pricing a product is how cheaply we can sell it"

The following statement made in 1953 is the only publicly available description of the ALDI system provided directly by the Albrecht brothers.[7]

"When I talk to you about pricing and about simplifying operations, I am telling you about my operation, how it works, because I believe that it is simple.

Today, in retrospect, I can say that we only stocked a small number of items out of necessity at the start of our development in 1948 and 1949. We were planning to open more outlets and had to be extremely frugal with our cash assets. We believed we would expand our product range later. We wanted our stores to be like other retail outlets, offering a wide range of groceries.

But we stayed as we were. We realized that we could still run a successful business with our narrow range of products and that, thanks largely to our narrow range of products, our expenses remained very low compared with those of other companies.

This insight became the basic principle of our business. Today, our costs stand at 11%.

Since 1950 we have adhered to the principle of low prices as well as that of limited selection. This was also a matter of necessity. If we did not want to offer customers a wide range then we had at least to offer them some other advantage. We sold our products for decisively less.

I am convinced that these two principles, narrow product range and low price, cannot be separated. Today, we can say that this policy has worked extremely well for us. In 1949 our average monthly turnover per store was DM 8,200, in 1951 DM 12,800, today it has reached DM 20,000 to DM 21,000.

This rise in turnover is due nearly exclusively to the principles I have just stated. Our expenditures on advertising do not even amount to 0.1%. All our promotional efforts are put into discount prices, and they are so effective that customers are even prepared to wait in line. At the weekend, lines nearly always form in front of the stores before they open. Not that business is only good at the weekend – early in the week, we also see good turnover figures.

At our strongest location, with a counter length of 5.5 m, we showed a turnover of DM 44,000 last month. At another location, with a counter length of 4 m, our turnover stood at DM 28,000.

To make this sort of performance physically possible, our shelves and counters are simply designed. The whole range of products is on counters or shelves where the customers can see it. There are no decorations in the stores.

Our product range amounts to about 250 to 280 items. We deliberately keep it small and under continual review. We take care that we do not offer similar items alongside each other. When we selected items for sale we went so far as to exclude whole product categories. The reason? Turnover.

Due to the throughput time we do not carry loose preserves, fruit or vegetables, or salted herrings, and because of the stock turn we do not carry preserved fruit or vegetables, delicatessen items such as mayonnaise, pickled fish, herring salad, etc. Our range of products is limited to consumer items that sell fast. We do carry loose legumes, but only one of each sort at any one time; one kind of beans or of lentils, and only one kind of rice, as well.

We do not carry packaged legumes, since the packaging costs would make the products too expensive for us and we would have to charge prices that would not fit into our pricing strategy. We have discovered that packaging goods in advance is often much more expensive than the total sum of our personnel costs. So we package nothing in advance [author's note: there was no self-service in 1953]. Everything must be weighed at the point of sale.

Further examples of our product range are:
- One type of sugar
- Four types of preserves in jars
- Five types of pasta which we always sell for the same price
- Five types of soap

The only shoe polish we carry is by Erdal, the only toothpaste is Blendax and the only floor wax in cans is by Sigella – these are leading German brands, and we always stick to the branded goods that sell the fastest. In the case of items with tight margins, too, such as oil, fat and lard, we only sell one kind. Extending our range and raising our costs is something we can do without.

Our policy on stock means selling is substantially easier and quicker for our sales personnel at the point of sale and that the customer can decide much more quickly – either to buy or not to buy.

In our pricing policy, we have fixed costing rates for many items. For the items with tight margins we apply these mark-ups:

Margarine	5–7%
Fat	10%
Bacon	10–12%
Lard	10%
Flour	10% maximum

When we sell oil, the cost price of a kilo is the retail price of a liter. That saves us working it out.

If purchase prices drop, we lower our sale prices immediately – even if we have yet to buy at the new prices. We take the position: offensive action is better than defensive action.

Maintaining a price when the purchase price has fallen is all very well in theory but is ultimately counterproductive. We want to convince our customers that they cannot buy things cheaper anywhere else. Once you have achieved that kind of goal – and I believe we have – your customers will put up with anything. They will even rearrange their schedules to come at the best shopping times.

In turn, this allows us to achieve nearly full utilization of our staff's capacity. This is the most important factor for low personnel costs – ours amount to between 3.1% and 3.7%.

This year, we have followed our principles with more rigor than ever before – and our results are all the better for it. In January, turnover stood at DM 250,000, in February DM 300,000, in March DM 340,000 and in April DM 394,000.

Our operation is directed almost entirely by the principle of low retail prices. No other measures are used to promote business; they are not even discussed. Our only consideration in pricing a product is how cheaply we can sell it, not how much people will pay for it."

Karl Albrecht made these statements of principle in 1953 when the ALDI concept did not involve self-service. Nonetheless, they remain as true now as then. Little, essentially, has changed – except, of course, that years of "intelligent refinement" have improved the cost ratio. Basically, a whole system was created by the accidental discovery that less really does mean more.

Less is more

Hard times and enforced frugality demanded the avoidance of waste. The principle was: less is better than too much. This applied to capital, personnel, floor space. The end result of this "poverty regime" was the ALDI concept. Shortage of resources inspired and created the idea of the century in retailing.

On May 11, 1980, in a letter to the editor of the authoritative German weekly trade magazine for the food industry, *Lebensmittel-Zeitung*, Karl H. Kuhlmann, at that time chairman of AVA/Marktkauf (today one of the largest retailers in Germany with a turnover of nearly euro 5bn) said ALDI was "the most successful food retailer of all time." The former Oetker director, Dieter Baader, a universally known expert in the German food industry and a frequent panel member at conventions, once told the Cologne/Bonn Marketing Club that: "ALDI is the greatest retail-policy driven brand success in the western world."

Groping forward in the dark

The ALDI concept was not based on any one specific corporate philosophy or on a strategic marketing study. It was more an adaptation to market forces and the competitive environment. The lessons learnt in the process were vigorously applied. The original concept remained, in essence, the same over the decades – changes were confined to incremental adjustments made in response to a wide range of internal and external developments. So it does not make sense to speak – as the trade papers sometimes do – of the old or the new strategies at ALDI.

The ALDI strategy was the result of a dynamic process, driven by intuition and decisions whose consequences were not always foreseeable. Starting out as a "Mom and Pop" store with a "simple, poverty-driven concept" it became, alongside Wal-Mart, the world's most successful retailer. As so frequently happens in business history, the beginnings were not an ingenious, academically reasoned design, but a good business idea that over the years developed into a solid foundation for success. The ALDI system was not a sudden invention. With their first "mini-stores in third-class locations" Karl and Theo Albrecht were literally groping their way forward to their sales system.[8] In this, they were not unlike Albert Einstein, who described his own way of proceeding as: "I grope my way forwards."

Recently, however, there have been the first indications, both internally and externally, of gradual change. There are signs that the product range is being widened – particularly at ALDI North. The "unbudgeable" and principled Mülheimers at ALDI South have only just begun – with great caution – to relax the rules.

But other changes are happening that are cause for concern. Business and leadership principles, however deeply rooted, do not always survive intact as decision makers and key actors change. At ALDI, a management team is in office that is clearly different from the managers of the 60s, 70s and 80s. In these years the mature concept was lived out and further refined. Asceticism, a low profile, attention to detail and incredible rigor were the essence of ALDI.

Theo Albrecht is handing over more and more responsibility to his sons. His once so stern authority and the loyalty to the principle demonstrated by the early members of the management and the administrative board appear to be declining in importance. That can mean important changes – especially for ALDI North. This book will point out these changes and the straws in the wind that indicate them in the appropriate context.

Yet the basic insights and methods presented in this book have been critical for the success of ALDI – and that of many other companies in many other industries as well. They remain in force and are becoming increasingly important at a time when many companies and in some cases whole industries are having to reorient themselves to face global competition. ALDI's insights and methods can help a number of companies become leaders in their sectors.

If the competition had paid closer attention to the words of Karl Albrecht, the retailing landscape might have looked altogether different. But even 30 years after 1953, there was still hardly anyone who believed in the success of the ALDI concept. In 1983 *Lebensmittel-Zeitung* came to the conclusion.

"Virtually no other marketing concept has been so thoroughly analyzed, or is so readily accessible – and yet practically a whole industry has watched the rise of the company . . . without doing anything and without a single creative response."[9]

But there was a lot more involved here than a "marketing concept." Those imitators who tried to copy ALDI apparently ran into the problem described by the poet Marie Ebner-Eschenbach (1830–1916): "Most imitators are attracted by what cannot be imitated."

The problem was that ALDI was much more than just a marketing concept. It was an operation founded on simplicity. People who tried to add to the original necessarily ran into difficulties, necessarily missed the point. The lesson? To paraphrase an old advertising copyline: "Beware of complex imitations."

Confidentiality on principle

There is very little known about ALDI. Thanks to its intelligent structure, because the organization is made up of many separate companies, privately owned ones at that, ALDI is not required to disclose its accounts. This obligation would be applicable if two of the three criteria of high turnover (at least euro 125m), a high number of employees (5,000 or over) and high total assets (euro 62.5m or over) were satisfied. In relation to confidentiality there are similarities with C&A, Ikea and, until recently, with the Metro Group. Like ALDI, these companies all have an outstanding concept, very individual corporate cultures, and all have sustained similar success over a long period.

ALDI has been discussed in a large number of newspaper articles. Competitors, market analysts and brand manufacturers have tried to find out more about the company in image studies and highly confidential hush-hush discussions. In other words, all speculation. For ALDI these studies sometimes passed on to them by their suppliers or discussed in the trade journals, were a useful way of finding out more about their own market, their customers or about the opinions of suppliers and competitors, without having to spend any money. ALDI themselves never spent any money on market research. ALDI people thought about their customers needs and then pursued a suck-it-and-see policy. They acted on their feel for what customers might like, and never paid for expensive research.

Waiving publicity is a conscious choice and an integral part of company policy. It limits the competition's access to information. Now, however, anyone can find out the number of ALDI's stores. The addresses of all the stores can be downloaded from the Internet at *www.aldi.com*. If companies publicize their organizational solutions or shout about how they have achieved increases in turnover or high personnel productivity and low costs, they only benefit their rivals. Competitors can use the information to improve their own performance; that cannot be good for a company like ALDI. And it does not help ALDI's customers, either: they do not read the trade papers. All they want is good quality at low prices.

The criticism of ALDI's "lack of public control" – which periodically arises – overestimates its potential influence: the disclosure of company developments, by reporting them in newspapers for example, has never prevented large public companies from collapsing or from having internal problems. Let us not forget companies such as coop AG; Bremer Vulkan, Metallgesellschaft or, the most recent example of poor management at Consumer Cooperative Dortmund.

History and growth

In 1913, the parents of Karl and Theo Albrecht opened a small grocery store with 35 square meters of floor space in Essen. After their release from prisoner of war camp in 1946, the Albrecht brothers ran a business with 100 square meters in Schonnebeck, a suburb of Essen largely populated by miners. By 1950, this business had already grown into a small chain of 13 stores. At that time, of course, counter service was still provided. The real business operation, says Karl Albrecht, actually started in 1948; two years later, the principle of low prices was added to that of narrow product range. The first "genuine" ALDI in today's terms was opened in Dortmund in 1962 – a creation of Theo Albrecht in the north of Germany that was later adopted by his brother Karl.

In 1961, the brothers divided their little empire into their North and South business units. They preferred individual leadership to team leadership – a principle of decentralization that has had a decisive – and positive – impact on the Albrecht Group. The basic reason for the separation was that it eliminated the need for continuous agreement on all matters. But, of course, neither brother worked in a vacuum: all details and performance and cost figures were exchanged, the terms and conditions of various suppliers were compared and some purchasing negotiations were conducted jointly. The only matter not discussed by the brothers was the actual annual profits of their respective group.

Turnover and number of stores of the ALDI Group in Germany

Year	Turnover Euro millions	Number of stores	Monthly average turnover* Euro millions
1955	15	100	12,500
1975	3,000	1,000	250,000
1985	8,500	2,000	354,000
1995	14,500	3,000	402,500
2000	19,000	3,350	472,500

* Purely statistical. Source: Author assessment and analysis by trade journals.

In 2000, ALDI had some 3,000 stores outside Germany turning over roughly euro 9bn.

Clear structures

ALDI's corporate structure is not, as many people maintain, opaque. On the contrary, it is very transparent and very simple (as shown opposite).

ALDI's corporate structure

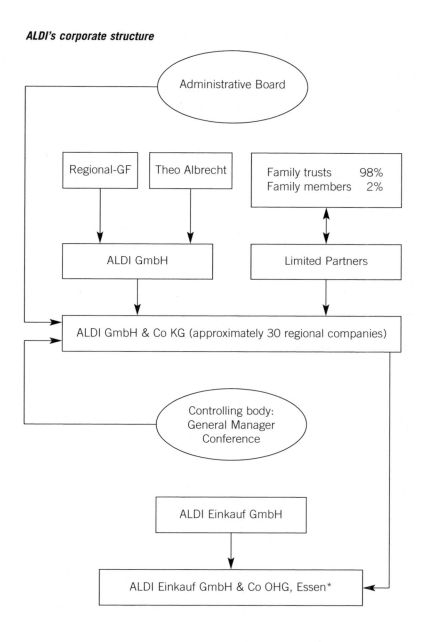

* In my chart – in contrast to the publications in the trade journals – ALDI Einkauf GmbH & Co OHG is demoted. It is in fact not a holding or parent company but a subsidiary that handles service functions for the ALDI companies, especially central buying.

The "unifier" as well as the management and control body of the group of companies is the administrative board that is made up of formally completely independent, self-employed managers who had previously been successful general managers of ALDI's regional companies. The members of the administrative board are not directors or employees of a parent or holding company. The administrative board acts as a supervisory board for each of the operating companies both within and outside of Germany.

There is no holding or umbrella company that controls other companies, which could lead to the legal constitution of a corporate group with all the related consequences, such as rights of workers to be involved in the management and accounting disclosure requirements. Since ALDI is not a corporate group in the conventional sense of the term, there is no corporate-level Works Council, elected by staff to represent employees' interests, either – a fact that was always criticized by the unions.

Critical for this structure is rigorous decentralization – a core principle of the ALDI corporate management.

ALDI (North)'s corporate structure

ALDI's corporate structure only appears complicated due to a large number of sole tradership, regional companies (ALDI North 36, ALDI South 30).

In addition to this basic set-up there is also a small number of important companies that is part of the group of companies: coffee processors in the towns of Herten/Westphalia and Weyhe near Bremen, the property development companies Albrecht Immobilienverwaltung GbR and A+G Grundstücksvermietungs und -verwaltungs GmbH, and the insurer Alva Versicherungsvermittlung GmbH & Co KG.

The establishment of the coffee processors and the Albrecht coffee brand was an early idea that turned out to be both profitable and image-forming. The coffee brand always enabled ALDI to demonstrate its high level of quality and its low prices particularly clearly. And coffee has remained the sole product that the company makes itself.

The property development companies facilitated the buying and management of property, the insurance company enabled them to cash in on the usual agent commissions for selling policies.

The structure of the family trust was chosen to protect and promote the interests of family members. Since a trust cannot be dissolved, the existence of the company is permanently assured, even in the case of family disagreements and inheritance battles. The family trust structure generally prevents protracted litigation leading to the dismemberment of companies. If two sons were sole heirs, they would each have a claim to half of the inheritance. But a company is a complex entity that cannot be simply cut in half like a bank account.

In ALDI, the family members – the parents Theo and Cilly as well as the sons Theo Jr and Berthold – only own a total of less than 40% of the company, so its continued existence is assured. Problems such as those recently seen at Bahlsen, a major producer of cookies in Hanover, can thus be avoided. At Bahlsen, interminable inheritance disputes could only be resolved by splitting off a substantial part of the company in the US and transferring it to one of the heirs.

The trust structure also puts many obstacles in the way of selling the corporate group to a third party. Walter Pellinghusen published a perceptive report on this subject in the August 13, 1998 issue of the German business weekly Wirtschaftswoche.

Financial development in Germany

The biggest question has always involved the profits ALDI makes. Many estimates have been made. Over the years, as the company grew into a major enterprise more and more details have been leaked, these have come increasingly closer to the truth. In an internal study, Lever estimated ALDI's profits for 1994 to be 4.5% of turnover, more than three times as high as the profit margin of competitors in the food retail business. The total costs of the company are estimated to come to 9%.

Monthly performance figures

Average turnover per store	euro 472,500
Turnover per employee	euro 75,000
Costs as a percentage of turnover	
Personnel costs of the stores	3.00%
Personnel costs for administration, logistics, management	2.50%
Rents of the stores	1.20%
Total costs of the company	10.00%
Gross profits as a percentage of turnover	
After value added tax	13.50%
Profit as a percentage of turnover	3.50%

From various reports published in the trade papers and from data that occasionally leak out to the media, ALDI's overall performance is as shown on the previous page. The relative sizes of the numbers in this chart are more remarkable than each individual figure.

ALDI's performance efficiency becomes clear if you consider that it only sells around 700 items, while Metro Cash & Carry or Rewe put at least 50,000 items on their shelves. Based on current statements and estimates of turnover in Germany – ALDI euro 17.5bn and Rewe euro 25bn – the average turnover per item per annum at ALDI comes out at euro 25m, at Rewe euro 0.5m.

And similar average turnover per item results using other assumptions and calculation methods.

Rewe's Food Turnover
euro 20bn from 20,000 items = euro 1.0m per item

Metro Cash & Carry's Food Turnover
euro 12bn from 15,000 items = euro 0.8m per item

These figures are not exact calculations – they are simply meant to give an idea of the scales involved. Rewe, including its distribution channels Minimal, Penny, Toom, HL and the independent Rewe purchasing agents, is probably the largest German food retailer measured by turnover. In terms of turnover per item, however, ALDI is 50 times bigger. The largest German retailer, Metro Cash & Carry, with a total turnover in Germany of euro 30bn, only sells euro 12bn's worth of food, and but that is based on maybe 15,000 items. These relative figures are why Klaus Jacobs, when speaking about the competitive coffee market in Germany in 1986, declared: "Our opponent is ALDI." And at that time Albrecht Coffee was sold in around 2,000 stores, while Jacob's coffee was sold in nearly every store, every convenience outlet and every gas station in Germany.

The famous ALDI profit margin of 4% is probably no longer achieved. And yet, the ALDI Group in Germany still turns in annual profits of roughly euro 0.65bn before taxes. These profits fluctuate less than those of major industrial companies such as Volkswagen or DaimlerChrysler – whose losses have, in some years, been in the billions.

The overall results of the ALDI Group have probably weakened over the past ten years. Competition has heated up considerably. Despite the strong expansion in non-food business and, most importantly, despite the recent expansion of the product range from 600 to 700 items at

ALDI North, turnover is likely to be stagnating at the North group in the states that made up former West Germany. Growth at present can only be seen from the opening of the new stores in the states of the former East Germany and from non-food promotions. Today, ALDI can achieve more than euro 200m in turnover just from a single sales campaign involving personal computers. ALDI South, which is traditionally one step behind in following the example of product range developments at ALDI North – refrigerated items, frozen foods, non-foods – may well have shown a somewhat better sales development. It only increased its number of items to 650.

Good grades from consumers and the trade journals

ALDI's success with consumers is remarkable – even to insiders. In 1996, research carried out by the popular German women's magazine *Brigitte* found that 55% of German consumers in the west and 44% of those in the east had a positive feeling about ALDI. For a no-frills discounter, this is an astonishing result. In contrast, the Rewe retail group only evoked positive feelings in 15% of those asked. Of those polled, 82% of westerners and 71% of easterners shopped at ALDI, while only 27% shopped at Rewe – until 1997, still the largest German retailer by turnover.

The good relationship with consumers was also reflected in a spontaneous poll, published in 1995 as part of the ALDI Study by the consumer research company Gesellschaft für Konsumforschung (GfK) in Germany. A few excerpts from this follow:

"ALDI is far and away the most well-known 'brand name' in German retailing." 56% of those polled thought first of ALDI when they were asked to name retail outlets. Edeka at 29%, Plus at 21%, Spar at 20% and Lidl at 18% were far behind.

"Consumers have the greatest confidence in ALDI." 26% spontaneously named ALDI as a retailer they had a great deal of confidence in, putting it clearly ahead of Edeka (13%), Plus (10%) as well as Spar (8%) and Lidl (6%).

"ALDI is not only low-price; it also provides good value for money." 46% gave "low prices" as a reason for shopping at ALDI, 44% praised the good value for money, clearing associating ALDI with quality.

"There are no clear negative points." Only 10% thought there were too few brand items and only 8% that there was too little choice. Only 5 to 7% complained about queues at the cash register, store design, product presentation or staff attitudes – common problems for most retailers.

"People of all classes and income brackets buy at ALDI." This was the perception of 48% of respondents. It is a finding that is repeatedly confirmed in other studies into how customers see themselves and fellow shoppers in their neighborhoods. 90% of all respondents said they shopped at ALDI.

"10 to 15% 'must' buy at ALDI." The study estimates the share of ALDI customers with large households, households including children, and bargain-hunting households to be from 10 to 15% of households in Germany. This group of "must-ALDI shoppers" will continue to grow.

"ALDI has a significant influence on overall pricing policy trends in food retailing." The market is ALDI price oriented. Even industry designs its production in part correspondingly. In 1981, selected brand goods were nearly twice as expensive as comparable ALDI items (96% higher in price). In 1994, the brands were only 74% more expensive. ALDI has not raised its prices; the others have adjusted their prices down.

ALDI's powerful credibility is based in no small part on the sensible idea of saving money. "People who don't hate their money," said Theo Albrecht, "can safely go shopping at ALDI." When he was finance secretary, Helmut Schmidt, as part of a meeting of G7 finance ministers, invited fellow ministers to his weekend house at Brahm Lake in Schleswig-Holstein. Televised reports showed a row of ALDI own labels on the Schmidt bar: the future Chancellor had bought them himself at the local ALDI market in Nortorf. Although champagne and smoked salmon are now available at ALDI, some customers still feel they have to emphasize that they are not ashamed of shopping there.

ALDI is not only rated well by customers, the experts give it good grades, too. In a study of crisis susceptibility published in *manager magazin* in February 1992, companies were assessed on a scale from 0 (least risk) to 100 (greatest risk). The sample was drawn from the ten largest industries in German and consisted of 66 companies, 7 of which were retailers.

The results were:

1	Deutsche Bank	30.83
2	Metro Cash & Carry	30.83
3	ALDI	31.50
4	Nestlé	33.50
5	Otto Versand	36.00
6	Phillip Morris	36.67

It is interesting to note the individual good marks given to ALDI:

Business risk	1st place
Market risk	2nd place
Financial risk	5th place

The assessment of ALDI's financial risk is certainly on the conservative side. It does not take into account that the group has, for many years, shown pre-tax earnings of some euro 0.5bn and that it counts substantial mortgage-free property holdings among its assets. It is even claimed that the ALDI company is Germany's largest property owner. It is certainly true that it is one of the larger real estate owners.

For years, ALDI has also received lavish praise in the annual image studies conducted by manager magazin. In 2002, ALDI ranked 13th among German companies as a whole, higher than such blue-chip organizations as Deutsche Bank, IBM, Nestlé or Airbus.

ALDI and the competition

How did ALDI's market position develop – both nationally and across Europe? ALDI has not pursued a policy of aggressive acquisition, of snapping up the opposition. Any predatory behavior has amounted to little more than the acquisition of other companies as vehicles for entering a few national markets outside Germany, and the takeover candidates were generally small. For ALDI South, the chosen vehicles were Hofer in Austria and Benner Tea in the US. For ALDI North, they were Combi in the Netherlands and Lansa in Belgium – acquisitions in which I was deeply involved.

Over the years, ALDI's market position has repeatedly been attacked by competitors. Besides ALDI, the leading companies in the discount sector in Germany currently include Lidl, Penny, Netto, Norma – Plus might rejoin the list in the near future. Lidl & Schwarz from Neckarsulm, with a pan-European turnover of euro 12.5bn in 1998, including some euro 5bn of discount turnover in Germany, and Penny/Rewe, with their discount turnover of some euro 4.5bn, are especially serious competitors.

Tengelmann gave up its attempt to put forward a new discount concept, "Ledi." Ledi was integrated into Plus, and Plus is supposed to become a new "tougher" discount model – like ALDI or Lidl. Tengelmann apparently failed in the past because its policies were only half-hearted. Commitment to principle is the quality that provided the foundation for ALDI's expertise.

The rapid development of discounting in Germany can be seen from the growth in the number of stores:

	1974	2000		1974	2000
ALDI	1,000	3,350	Plus	180	2,900
Penny	60	2,500	Norma	190	1,100
Lidl	10	2,000	Netto	0	800

Discount stores account for around 30% of total food retail turnover. According to statistics from the umbrella organization of German retailing, Hauptverband des Deutschen Einzelhandels (HDE), the total turnover in German food discount stores amounted to euro 36bn in 1996. In 1995, 88% of the people living in Germany said they bought in discount stores; by 1996, this figure had risen to 93%. Another study revealed that 72% of consumers shopped at least occasionally at ALDI. For the competitors, these values were substantially lower in relation to their corresponding market shares: Plus 33%, Lidl 28%, Penny 23%.

ALDI's current market share – in the "relevant" market – is vastly underestimated at 13%. For all the food retailers active in the German retail market the following figures can be assumed for 2000.

Total food turnover	euro 115.0bn
Food turnover of the 30 largest companies	euro 107.5bn
60% of the food turnover may be said to consist of the product range that ALDI sells, which means:	
ALDI "relevant" food turnover	euro 70bn*
ALDI turnover of directly comparable goods	euro 50bn*
(for example, the small range of packaged cheeses sold at ALDI)	

* Author's estimate.

Therefore, ALDI's share of the German food retail market is 38%. In other words, more than every third German euro, when comparable product ranges are taken into account, is spent by consumers at an ALDI cash register.

ALDI's importance is further underlined by its market shares for individual items and product categories. Here are a few examples:[10/11]

Product Category	Market Share
Fruit juices	51%
Preserved vegetables	42%
Processed meat and sausage	50%
Preserved fruit and vegetables	30%

Even in the market for personal computers, ALDI is already coming close to a 10% share. And ALDI is increasingly important as a retail outlet for textiles.

"ALDI is where the action is"

In the early years of rapid expansion in particular, ALDI had frequently to do battle with local authorities, especially in smaller towns. When new sites were in the planning stage local retailers often complained to the local authorities that were in charge of issuing permits. Frequently, the retailer was also a member of the town council. People were afraid that the giant ALDI would destroy the infrastructure of the local retailers and put local corner stores to the wall by undercutting their prices.

But, over time, this attitude has changed: developments did not at all confirm these fears. ALDI attracted more customers to the area, and its narrow product range gave other retailers sufficient room for maneuver. If the competitors adapted to the situation intelligently they found themselves better off than they were before. Like all other vendors, they had to ask the question: "Why should customers come to my store?" Specialized retailers such as butchers or green grocers like to be close to ALDI. And it is virtually never the other way round, as is often assumed.

This unexpected development has been reflected in the media. For example, the *Goslarsche Zeitung*, a local paper, discussed an ALDI opening by writing: "For the city, the opening of the ALDI market . . . means that the goal has been achieved. It is common knowledge that ALDI, as a narrow-range retailer with around 650 items, in contrast to full-line retailers carrying 3,000 to 5,000 items, tends to support, not threaten, local food retailers." The German national weekly Stern once quoted the spokesman of the Edeka headquarters in Hamburg as saying: "ALDI is where the action is."

Is the end of growth in sight?

The impressive ALDI growth statistics give rise repeatedly in the trade journals to speculation on whether this progress can go on. Many believe that unless changes are made, the end is near. Both knowledgeable trade journalists and industry insiders share this idea, hoping of course that soon everything will return to normal, that both their personal view of the world and the traditional path of corporate development will apply once again, and that competitors will be doing much better. All are agreed that, since growth is vitally important to ALDI, the company must expand its product range – for example, include meat – and make many other changes.

But ALDI's policy has, historically, been to change the composition of its range rather than the number of items it sells. It has moved with the market – and moved with the times. Once whole coffee beans, women's stockings and records were sold – items for which demand is no longer high. They have been replaced by everyday goods that were once difficult to carry but are now easy to handle – for example, dairy products and frozen foods.

The most significant widening of the range has happened over the past ten years with the expansion of non-food items and additional fruits and vegetables. These changes in the product range could not be made before a certain level of turnover had been reached and all the related logistical questions had been answered.

It is only in the last two years that ALDI has shown the first signs of creeping uncertainty. When people are so used to success they find it difficult to accept stagnation. The competitive pressure in the discount business has increased, more and more retailers, including the newcomer Netto, are entering the market, and Lidl has been continuously strengthening its position. This has had a negative impact on turnover increases and, finally, led to the – admittedly limited – product range expansion from 600 to 700 items at ALDI North.

Among the many misjudgments made about ALDI is a 1977 analysis carried out by market researcher G+I Forschungsgemeinschaft für

Marketing: "The turnover growth of roughly 15% in 1975 can essentially be put down to a product-range expansion by the Albrecht outlets." From the same source comes the finding: "For the first time in 1975 ALDI itself must accept falling turnover, lost particularly to other discounters (like Norma, Penny, Plus and so on) who basically are copying the Albrecht principle."

An individual store is nearly always affected by a new, nearby store – at least when it first opens – but apart from that, the assumptions that ALDI could not maintain its market position and its growth have nearly always turned out to be wrong, based more on hope than reality. Trade journalists and retail analysts want to be read by other retailers, and good tidings are always more welcome than news that compels people to think and – more importantly – to think again.

Part 1
The ALDI corporate culture

The corporate culture is the key to success

"What is essential is invisible to the eye." This observation by Saint-Exupéry is probably the best way of summing up ALDI's secret. What is visible – store decorations, product ranges and prices – have been easily copied by competitors. It is the invisible that has determined ALDI's success. To understand the company, you must understand the essential, defining characteristics that lie beneath the surface.

In this chapter, I will be dealing with one of the most important aspects of the ALDI success story: standards and values – the corporate culture.

The cultural rules viewed collectively work in many communities almost like laws – frequently even better. Cultural rules guide how members think, feel and behave. They are frequently passed on in subtle ways to new members of the organization and to subsequent generations. People are always looking for guidance and they find it in unwritten sources as well as in the literal rulebook. Cultural rules give each company its own, unique identity.

The corporate culture influences the attitudes of employees toward their work, the product and the company. There are few principles that will make a company and its employees successful, but a special culture will do it. There are only few principles, but the culture that leads the company and its employees to success is special. Standards and values determine the personality of a company.

Such standards and values can be official and explicit or even formulated in writing. However, they may also be present in the company but operate in unwritten form. Companies develop ways of working that are specific to them, that make it clear to employees what the company considers "good" or "bad," "permitted" or "forbidden," what it "rewards" and what it "punishes."

Once asked at the German Trade Congress about the culture of his company, AVA manager and market purchasing boss Helmut Kohlwes gave a refreshingly clear, honest and practical answer: "Corporate culture, hmmm, what is ours, actually?" There is a lot to say about culture at ALDI, but ALDI employees would probably have responded in the same way as Kohlwes.

Unwritten rules

A corporate culture feeds on examples and role models, on the special "characters" of the company, especially the founders and owners. Theo and Karl Albrecht are just such "characters," standing for the corporate culture that they endorse. ALDI is decisively shaped by its founders, and this is probably why attempts to copy the company have been doomed to failure.

The cultural values and rules have never been officially formulated at ALDI and put down in writing. The only exception is the objective set in job descriptions: "Our competitive edge must be retained by applying the principle of economy in its extreme form." Since ALDI only has unwritten rules in the first place nobody could contradict the "secret rules" so often mentioned in business literature which in reality assured the survival of the company. However, we can assume that any official rules would have been unlikely to contradict the "secret" ones.

You do not need written rules to have clarity of purpose. Of course, friction can arise between individuals and divert their energies. ALDI is a company like any other, in which real people with their individual strengths and leadership weaknesses work so that some conflict is inevitable. The key thing is that everyone knows the drill.

To reinforce a specific culture in a company, the role models and the examples set by the owners and managers are very important. Equally important, however, is whether the cultural rules – those precepts considered important – are repeatedly made a subject of discussion.

What the company's managers focus their attention and activities on is significant. It leaves its mark. Leaders need to check consciousness-raising by asking themselves questions such as: Are matters of cultural relevance repeatedly put on the agenda of meetings? How much time are they given? Another important point is what management looks for in employees, locations or departments. This form of control is an extraordinarily important, practical leadership instrument for any boss.

Culture must not be mechanically or routinely placed on the agenda, without motivation, or simply form part of a defined control program. No, what is decisive is that these things are done simply because a compulsion, a need, a certain passion for good results requires that certain subjects be repeatedly made the focus of attention.

Agendas and control programs reflect the "cultural requirements" at ALDI to a large extent. But this is also due to the fact that the cost consciousness which forms part of the organization's culture is always a practical, topical item'. Perhaps this is even typical of culture: it happens and is important, non-stop, every day.

"In the end there is no control more effective than a distinctive, homogeneous corporate culture. If the general direction is right, the details can be entrusted to decentralized self-organization. Time-consuming co-ordination and control systems can be dropped."

These words, taken from the book *Managing Corporate Change*, by the management experts Klaus Doppler and Christoph Lauterburg, could have been written with ALDI in mind. The company's organization, with its decentralized leadership, is based on this culture.

In terms of culture, there is consistency between all ALDI regional companies. As Peter Drucker has recommended: "Decisive for a good organization is that everyone is playing the same tune."

Of course, this also includes job descriptions that are short and precise and followed faithfully by the individual employees, as well as a sophisticated control system in the form of spot checks. Co-ordination is rarely necessary under these conditions. Even if employees at ALDI see the control system as too extensive, it has a different scope and above all quality from those in many other companies. This will be discussed in greater detail in the section entitled "The principles of delegation and control."

Culture by example

An important part of the control system is "cultural control." This primarily involves finding out whether supervisors convey the values and rules of ALDI to their employees. For the ALDI system to work, managers have to live up to the highest standards. Credibility, achieved by agreement between what managers say and what they do, is one of the secrets. And doing means setting an example. Theo Albrecht is known by everyone as someone who turns off the light when he enters a room to save on electricity if – in his opinion – there is enough light without it. This is a small but, paradoxically, illuminating example, one which wouldn't have any effect if he and others did not behave in exactly the same way in other, similar situations.

The following quotations encapsulate this success factor.

*"Explanations are the long way 'round,
teaching by example is quick and effective."*
Seneca

"Examples guarantee success."
Bertolt Brecht

The main cultural rules are observed by virtually all the employees and closely adhered to by the supervisors. The rules are so well established that exceptions to them are quickly recognized.

Helmut Maucher, for many years the CEO and leading policy maker at Nestlé, has cited ALDI as proof that a company's corporate culture and public image are intimately related. Somehow people know what Siemens, Otto-Versand or ALDI represent, people have a picture of the employees and their behavior.

Graham Seabrook, the head of the UK discount chain Kwik Save, has drawn attention to the relationship between cultural rules and success.

"I believe that culture is probably the most important critical success factor contributing to sales of discount foods. The switch from high-profit–margin thinking to discount approach requires a certain degree of adaptation. And some people simply cannot change their ways of thinking because they grew up in another culture. Tesco is an example which proves that the discount concept cannot possibly work if management is not absolutely convinced of it."

So what are the typical values and rules at ALDI? Drawing in particular on the insights I acquired during the 10 years I worked alongside Theo Albrecht, I will attempt to describe and comment on the ALDI corporate culture. I call this an attempt because some aspects of the culture are changing and therefore cannot, with complete confidence, be identified fully or correctly, and also because perception is always subjective. The definition of what I consider to be "relevant to culture" in individual cases plays a role as well. It should also be noted that ALDI North and ALDI South differ in some respects, though not in essentials.

Asceticism as a basic principle

According to Ghandi, "asceticism is the highest of the arts" and "a true ascetic does not simply practice his art, he lives it." Schopenhauer even thought that "all conceivable future problems can be overcome by means of asceticism." He judged asceticism to be a "cure for everything." Of course, that may be an exaggeration. But I would put asceticism at the top of the list of cultural values at ALDI. Asceticism in the sense of doing without is, I believe, the most important core characteristic of the company. Theo Albrecht once said: "People live more on what they do not eat."

An overview of ALDI produces a doing-without checklist:

The doing-without checklist
1   No staff to relieve management of intellectual work
2   No controlling department to provide direction
3   No external market research
4   No work with management consultants
5   No budget forecasts
6   No scientifically cleaned statistics that reveal all
7   No scientific analysis techniques for all questions related to supplying the market
8   No customer surveys
9   No ISO 9000 or TQM
10 No sophisticated system of terms and condition to squeeze supplier prices
11 No differentiated price policy by sales area or store type
12 No differentiated product mix from store to store
13 No complicated calculation methods for setting prices
14 No games involving qualities to optimize profits
15 No highly complicated engineering for logistics
16 No product placement in stores based on psychological analysis of shopper behavior
17 No luxury in the offices, no top-of-the-range company cars
18 No public appearances
19 No publicity
20 No acceptance of gifts from suppliers
21 No acceptance of invitations to dinner from suppliers

The ALDI stores have simple, even spartan interiors. Telephones were rejected on the grounds that they were not absolutely necessary and would significantly increase costs. It was not until data cash registers were installed that the idea of the telephone became sensible. The break rooms for personnel, with simple tables and chairs, were not especially comfortably furnished. Working conditions like these – frequently including pressure to perform quickly – are not everyone's idea of a dream job.

Logically enough, these circumstances are also considered when designing the workplaces in the central offices and planning management's working environment. Simple and functional furniture is chosen. The company cars are not especially luxurious. The directors drive the smallest model in the Mercedes S class, without any extras – no metallic paints, just standard colors. This was true for decades.

One could almost forget that this is by far the best-earning company in its sector in Germany. If you compare the cost of managerial staff and offices at competing companies that earn a fraction of the ALDI profits, the cultural differences appear even more stark. I think this is one factor – if not the biggest factor – behind the major differences in the annual statements.

ALDI has always been conspicuous by its low profile and this is, appropriately, reflected in the most important part of the company, the stores. This is where business takes place, this is where most of the employees work. The factor of credibility cannot be underestimated. ALDI's outlets have much in common with Metro Cash & Carry outlets. Anyone could recognize the shared characteristics: simply and functionally arranged sales rooms, sparely equipped offices – throughout the management hierarchy. The long-standing head of Metro, Erwin Conradi, had an even simpler office than Theo Albrecht. And he was always visible to his employees: his office walls were made of glass.

ALDI operates a clearly ascetic sales concept – spartan store design with a simple product range developed to meet the basic needs of the consumer. Until very recently, luxury items such as champagne and smoked salmon were only available in the weeks before Christmas. The emphasis is on the prosaic – preserved foods, jellies, long-life milk, detergents, toilet paper.

Frugality as a guiding principle

ALDI's low profile goes hand-in-hand with frugality and extreme cost consciousness. This is evident not only in instructions given to employees but in a determined, ongoing effort at all levels to avoid unnecessary costs. Consider Theo Albrecht's good examples of using both sides of sheets of paper and of turning the light off when there is enough light from outside.

By continually improving lamp design and lux values in the stores power was also saved. The significance of the original decision to do without telephones becomes clear when one considers the following calculation: if you assume that unnecessary telephone calls, excessively long conversations and personal calls add up to 50 euros per month in one store, then the figure for 3,000 stores is 1.8 million euros annually.

The principle of frugality is not, of course, confined to the day-to-day running of the stores. It affects all areas of the business. There have been attempts to use retread tires whose tread can be recut to prolong the life of company trucks. Wind deflectors have been added to the front of trucks to reduce wind resistance and thus cut fuel consumption. Frugality is also the prime concern in the development of new warehousing and freight shipping techniques. ALDI has developed a system that allows three pallets to be transported simultaneously by forklift trucks. In a cooperative effort with suppliers, ideal box sizes were established, eliminating the frequent need to cut boxes. Cooperative projects to design the best boxes now come under a more scientific and important designation in the industry, "efficient consumer response" (compare this with the section entitled "Success is not decided by purchasing but by the marketing concept").

Frugality calls into question even things that are normally taken for granted – for example, whether membership of an association of retailers, which costs money, is really necessary.

These are just a few indications of a clearly focused behavior pattern that is followed by many employees, managers and departments. Each effort, each solution is a manifestation of the guiding principle and an endorsement of the corporate values of economy, waste avoidance and extreme cost consciousness.

"Muda," the Japanese word for waste that is so popular today, had never been heard of at ALDI when it made economy part of daily working life. ALDI people have always put effort into dropping unproductive ways of working. These examples also illustrate the obsession with detail that is discussed later.

When I flew to America to supervise the purchase of stakes in Albertson's (Boise, Idaho) and in Trader Joe's (Los Angeles), ALDI bought me a first-class ticket. It was the greatest luxury I had experienced at the organization – and the flights were between 11 and 13 hours long. Compared with their peers, the family that owns ALDI live simply. Until he was kidnapped, Theo Albrecht drove his own car, a relatively modest sedan. His office is simply equipped. No one could possibly accuse him of profligacy. Many other companies and managers, by contrast, spare no expense when it comes to design and luxury.

Promoting managers from within

Keeping a low profile does not only mean doing without luxury and status symbols but also the way people behave and relate to each other. Even when talent hunting, whether for the purpose of recruitment or promotion, ALDI is looking for managers who are modest as well as good and therefore fit into the corporate culture.

Since people are generally vain, this modesty and asceticism are probably only sustained because the individual can take pride in his or her achievements and in a company that outshines the competition. Secretly, ALDI people know success is on a completely different scale.

Self-discipline is also a necessary and typical quality of ALDI executives – one that promotes the company's core cultural values and rules of frugality, publicity shyness and fairness toward others, especially suppliers.

Practising this type of asceticism day on day is no small feat, and there are some who fail completely at it. This has always provided cogent arguments for recruiting trainee managers from within the company. ALDI's executives, in general, have come up through the ranks, through the various departments in sales and supply chain management. Among today's regional managers, for example, you can find former district managers, sales managers, administrative managers, distribution center managers and even store managers.

These trainee managers know the organization, the "front line," and have been initiated into the corporate culture early on. To ALDI, the right character is generally more important than, say, a degree from Harvard: none of our executives is from McKinsey; none boasts any other kind of exclusive background.

> *"Human behavior and strategy must conform to each other."*
> Rolf Berth

Strategy and character are inextricably linked; no personality type can follow more than a very limited number of strategic concepts. The ALDI strategy is so special that not everyone would fit into it easily. The management consultant Rolf Berth studied a large number of companies[12] and concluded that a strategic concept can only be implemented effectively by the right personalities – failures, botched enterprises, bankruptcies are largely down to discrepancies between the tasks on the agenda and character. I believe ALDI has largely succeeded in bringing these two into sync.

No gossip, no scandals

Former Volkswagen senior manager Daniel Goeudevert, who has become a best-selling author with his book *Like a Bird in an Aquarium*, inveighs against developments that cause them not to keep their feet on the ground and makes them complacent. The danger of top managers and politicians, attempting to promote themselves and their social status by making high-profile appearances, thereby neglecting the company's interests, is now commonly acknowledged.

Among ALDI executives, however, the risk of this sort of behavior is slight. There are no precedents for it. The Albrechts have never permitted their managers to appear in public as "emperors with no clothes." They also shun the limelight themselves. *Forbes* magazine once said that there have been more sightings of the Yeti than of Theo Albrecht.

That public appearances of ALDI managers in their professional capacity are unacceptable is an unwritten rule. Interviews focused on ALDI issues are strictly prohibited, even if they would clearly benefit the company or be promotional in nature. They do not reflect the company's style, set by the good example of the owners. This is because there is a fear that they do not protect the company's interests. There is a fear that someone could say too much. Good journalists have clever ways of asking questions.

Just for a moment, consider how much time some executives spend making presentations, giving interviews, writing articles, taking part in panel discussions. Does that help their company? Generally, the answer has to be no. For banks, management consultants and lawyers, things may be different: their customers may well be in the audience. For retailers, the real audience, the shopper, is somewhere else.

What you frequently see in corporate events is sheer "muda," waste. The worst kind of profligacy often occurs at public liability/joint stock companies, which find it all too easy to spend other people's money, the funds of anonymous shareholders.

A culture of asceticism like ALDI's is often accompanied by impersonal management. Large gatherings such as Christmas parties or company parties are rare. This is sometimes to the regret of employees, but the impersonal style is an integral part of ALDI culture.

Again and again the press, especially, of course, writers from the trade journals, have been keen to penetrate the largely "unknown ALDI company." Everyone knew the stores but very few people knew anything about the people who ran them. The unknown makes people insecure, secretive behavior makes them suspicious. But the search for the journalistic hook, for that bit of private gossip, has remained unsuccessful. For many years, there have been no scandals at ALDI, no stories about skeletons in the family closet. The birth of quadruplets to Berthold Albrecht hit the headlines of German's most popular daily tabloid, *Bild*, but that was about all. There has been no reason for bad press. The closest comparison that can be drawn with ALDI on this point until recently was C&A Brenninkmeijer, however, this company did draw media attention to itself largely due to the secretive behavior of the family clan.

The only spectacular event in the history of ALDI has been the kidnapping of Theo Albrecht, the first professionally organized kidnapping in Germany.

In December 1971, Theo Albrecht was abducted from the ALDI site in Herten, Westphalia. After finishing work, he was heading for his car to drive himself home (as always he had no chauffeur.) He was kidnapped and held hostage at an address in a busy Dusseldorf street. Initially, in the company, word went out that he was home with a cold. It was a pretty feeble explanation for his absence: it was unusual for him to have a cold in any case, and as far as anyone could remember, he had never had a day's sick leave in his life. A ransom of 3.5m euros was paid for his release, 2m euros of which remains unaccounted for. At that time, it was the highest ransom that had ever been paid in Germany.

Quiet success

Competitors were blind to the development of ALDI. To this day, even trade journals barely know who the members of the company's management are. The reputable German trade journal for the food industry, *Lebensmittel-Zeitung*, was, until a few years ago, unable to distinguish between Essen and Mülheim, the respective headquarters of the North and South divisions. Today, quite a bit is known about ALDI. In the 1970s and 1980s, a period of significant growth, however, there was much misreporting. ALDI did not mind: imitators were frequently misled by the trade journals.

In 1976, at the AIDA congress in Geneva, Bernt Lietke from *Lebensmittel-Zeitung* gave a lecture about the "Albrecht Concept." Some of what he said was accurate, but many of the details were wrong.

The incorrect statements included:

- "If Albrecht is undercut, the item in question is eliminated from the product range."
- "Priority is given to sticking to a small number of suppliers."
- "Long-term agreements are made."
- "The goal of low rents no longer applies, the best locations are looked for."
- "Albrecht is having difficulties with slower growth and market share losses in some categories."

These statements were a consolation for the competition and benefited ALDI: the company could afford to continue growing at a leisurely pace. ALDI's low profile, its policy of not saying too much, and above all of not talking publicly about its almost legendary success had a lot to do with this.

"Best regards from Mülheim"

In those days, I found even the mention of my name in an issue of the prominent German marketing monthly *absatzwirtschaft* in 1976 unpleasant when I, as a member of the administrative board, was quoted as having said the non-committal and banal sentence: "Potential growth from opening new locations naturally becomes limited as the density of outlets increases."

A statement issued by Mülheim (Karl Albrecht's ALDI South) was even terser: responding to a question from *Wirtschaftswoche* regarding a test result published by the German consumer protection association *Stifting Warentest* (the subject of the test: laundry detergent), in which ALDI had once again received a good review, the written answer was: "Our company does not provide any figures or other information to the public whatsoever as a matter of principle. Best regards."

Public relations has hardly ever become an issue for ALDI. The kidnapping was one exception. A dispute about the fact that, around 20 years ago, cashiers had no conveyor belts and had to check goods through by moving them from one shopping trolley to another, shifting tons of goods every day with only one hand. This attracted massive public criticism – led, in large part, by the unions. Although the discussion did not deal adequately with the actual conditions, after intensive investigation ALDI was finally prepared to change working conditions.

After a long debate, ALDI may have acted on its own conviction, but this was also in response to public pressure. The issue was solved by being proactive, and conveyor belts were introduced to make cashiers' work easier and, possibly, to even speed up the flow of goods at the cash register.

The disturbing side of the debate with the labor union HBV (Commerce, Banking and Insurance) and the Institut für Arbeitswissenschaften (Institute of Labor Studies) in Dortmund was that the discussions were extremely emotional. Once the notion was accepted that physical work, which was often related to years of training, was not basically damaging, the unbalanced nature of the work was subsequently bemoaned. The question is then, which profession is not affected by unbalanced activity. Anyone who works with his hands, house-painters for example, perform activities which are unbalanced. The discussion about the extent to which cashiers' illnesses were psychosomatic or due to the extremely unbalanced physical work was also very emotional. I believe unions and employers can learn from these discussions that open co-operation can provide good solutions better and more quickly than emotional debates.

The principle for dealing with the public, especially with the trade journals, was: what we do, we do for our customers. For this purpose we do not need journals that are read by curious competitors. What we might say there can only be of use to the competition. Here too, ascetic behavior plays a role: stick to what is important for achieving business goals. What remains is the pride in producing excellent performance in an interesting job. This is the source of genuine motivation. Quietly, without distractions, people can be much more effective. The unique success and the strict avoidance of publicity are the two sources that fed the "ALDI myth."

The ALDI characteristics of reticence and discretion have, as I have said, stood the company in good stead. They have certainly made life difficult for competitors that wanted to imitate the ALDI way, copy our success. Lidl has, after many failed attempts, at last succeeded in replicating all ALDI's visible characteristics – even the floor tiles and the longer customer lines at the cash registers are "ALDI like" – but it has yet to get the essentials right. Imitating the visual aspects of a store is not enough. Lidl needs to improve its product-range policy. There are secrets behind the scenes, and an uncompromising determination to follow policies with the utmost rigor. That is where the invisible culture comes into play.

No manipulation – no tricks

ALDI has always used the scope in the tax and statutory regulations, and still does so. There has never been any attempt to ignore or evade statutory regulations. How can you expect your employees to behave correctly if you set a poor example?

Labor laws are observed at ALDI. ALDI has always attempted to win recognition for their own opinions on labor law in their difficult disputes with works councils, both with the support of experts and in the labor courts. I believe this is right, as long as the disputes do not simply involve tilting at windmills. For example, the bonus system for sales assistants is based on the monthly performance of the whole store, the monthly turnover being divided by the number of hours worked. The better the performance, the higher the bonus. The attempt had been made to exclude employees from the premium plan to a limited extent who were absent due to illness. Because when someone is missing, the premium not only goes up for those on the job, but also for the absentee, since usually no substitute can be found for several days. The attempt was thus made to eliminate the nonsense that people could earn more by being absent due to illness. But on this point ALDI did not convince the court, and paid up honestly, without resorting to tricks.

Another example is the years of discussion about hiring part-timers. The unions called the women workers at ALDI the "call girls" of retailing because they were phoned when stores needed additional personnel. The system of adapting the number of personnel to fluctuating turnover was called "Kapovaz," an acronym formed from the German words meaning capacity-oriented variable working hours. Adjusting costs to turnover is a legitimate goal for all companies and, in the end, ALDI succeeded in defending its approach.

The dispute benefited employees by resulting in agreements between ALDI management and the Works Council that protected employees from unreasonable demands. Employees cannot be compelled to leave their homes if, for example, they are in the middle of cooking a meal. There has to be a schedule they can organize their time around.

The terms of contractual, legal and collective bargaining agreements are adhered to rigidly – an approach which is difficult for many companies due to the unchecked expansion of social and protective laws. ALDI attempted, as mentioned above, to influence the rate of absenteeism due to illness using a bonus system, but this was not tenable from a legal point of view and had to be dropped, to the regret of the creative authors of this system.

Fair treatment of suppliers

Despite numerous press reports to the contrary, the principle of correct and fair treatment is clearly reflected in ALDI's relationships with its suppliers. Over the years, complaints by suppliers dismissed on the grounds of poor quality and false assumptions made by so-called industry experts have fuelled stories of intimidation, dependence, and abuse of power. They are not true. That is not the ALDI way.

According to the industry information service, Extrakte: "Albrecht not only make their payments so promptly that you can set your clock by them, they are also fair partners."

Correct practice also includes the rejection of bribery. A bottle of champagne at Christmas may seem like an innocent enough gift but the giver has an ulterior motive. There is no such thing as a free gift. Any supplier who genuinely wanted to show their appreciation would remember the sales assistants, not just the purchasing agent. Everyone in the industry knows how imaginative suppliers can be in their attempts to keep buyers on side. The ultimate blandishment may even be a VW convertible for the buyer's spouse or a luxury holiday in Portugal.

Such practices are widespread but that does not mean they should be accepted as a fact of life. While I was working in Turkey, I was offered three all-expenses-paid weeks at the Olympic Games in Atlanta. A popular beverage manufacturer wanted this gesture to leave a good and lasting impression. It was disappointed, though: I declined the invitation.

One ALDI central purchaser alone negotiates annual volumes worth roughly 1 to 2.5bn euros. When the sums are this large, generous "presents" are peanuts. The dangers are great for all retail businesses, and there is virtually no completely foolproof protection for the company. To take bribes, however, is to compromise one's integrity. At ALDI, it results in dismissal.

ALDI has a clear regulation: the biggest present that may be accepted is a calendar. Anything else is turned down and returned with a friendly note and a request for appreciation of the writer's position. All invitations to lunch and dinner must be rejected. ALDI staff pay inspection visits to manufacturer's headquarters but that is all: they do not make social calls.

Customers can have complete confidence

"Anyone who is useful to someone else is useful to himself."
Seneca

Customer orientation is the new buzzword of marketing. Related terms such as "clienting," "customizing," "customer management, "efficient consumer response," "customer focusing," "earnings-oriented management of customer satisfaction," "relationship management" are now in fashionable use.

At the heart of this jargon is the oldest "wisdom" in business: "The customer is king." Business is done with customers who normally are free to choose to buy or not to buy. In reality, this simple rule is sufficient but the textbooks and journals are full of "the latest, revolutionary insights" so it is necessary to disprove the theories by the ALDI example.

Simplicity is not easy

The case for customer orientation appears to be self-evident and simple – customers' needs are the obvious focus for company strategy. The problem is that few people are good at sticking to what is simple.

That is why consultants who can tell troubled executives something about "clienting" earn money. That is why the "translation of closeness to the customer into a complete management package" is demanded. That is why the reputable consultancy A. T. Kearney has even developed the concept of enterprise customer management (ECM).

Orientation toward the customer has become so complicated that even experienced managers are incapable of achieving it on their own. Too much time is being spent on theoretical treatises, too little on practical solutions. In the many words expended to state simple thoughts it is possible – to paraphrase Schopenhauer – to trace the unmistakable signs of mediocrity. Take the following:[13]

"The customer earnings statement is ultimately the difference between expenditures and net earnings from the exchange of goods and services, taking into account the individual customer relationship and dialog processes, and shows the current earnings value of the customer relationship. Earnings-oriented customer satisfaction management is focused on the evaluated future, or potential, earnings value of the customer relationship, taking into account the targeted and systematic shaping of specific customer relationships and dialogue processes on the basis of the target degree of customer

satisfaction that is deduced from the insights provided by the customer satisfaction analysis."

At ALDI, we consciously never made the effort even to begin to understand such ideas. This saved us a lot of time and permitted us to focus our attention on essentials – on the concrete, not the abstract. What would have become of ALDI if management had concentrated its efforts on these "fundamental, revolutionary insights"? There is a fitting response to the hot air of management speak: "If it sounds like nonsense, it usually is nonsense."

ALDI was and remains a success because of its focus on simple issues. As Tom Peters and Robert Waterman demand in their book *In Search of Excellence*, we went "back to basics." We realized the simple reality that expenditure can only be covered by customer sales. The customer pays for and finances everything. He pays the salaries, he pays the suppliers' bills, and he pays the taxes. In addition, he also – it is to be hoped – contributes to profits so that owners and shareholders can get some "fun" out of their efforts.

In 1995, at the annual convention of the MMM (Modern Market Methods) Club, Fredmund Malik, professor of business management at the University of St Gallen, formulated the answer to all basic questions:

"Improve value to the customer instead of merely concentrating on increasing profits."

The shortest path to recognizing customer needs

But what does the customer want? How can we find out? For a start, the senior manager has to come down from his Ivory Tower and visit his own stores. Market research and Nielsen data alone are not very helpful. Tests, surveys, listening, observing and sensitively stepping into the customer's shoes – being one's own customer – are what help. The easiest way to judge the performance of your own company is to buy your own products. For retailers, that means doing their own shopping. They must become their own customers – shopping with a list they have written at home and in a store where they are not recognized as a senior member of staff. You only notice the important details when you yourself are standing at the shelves.

I am not talking about hiring an army of paid shoppers from an outside company. Or about asking the wife of the head of purchasing to "do a bit of shopping." I am talking about the actual manager doing it. Before consulting experts, it is often enough to become aware of the experience we have ourselves as customers in all kinds of areas. This is the reality the management speak neglects.

Let's look now at customer orientation in action. Recently, I bought a three-volume work on Islam. Unfortunately, I left Volume II on the plane. The Heymann book store in Hamburg, where I had *not* bought the original set, told me that the volumes were not sold separately, but I did not want to fork out 45 euros for another full set. The bookstore offered to ask the publisher, Herder, whether it could make an exception. After two weeks, I received my missing volume – free of charge!

A retailer has, quite literally, to believe in its customers. Quibbling about service is not likely to get the customer on your side, win you their loyalty. This is, again, best seen if you put yourself in the customer's shoes. Suppose you buy a sofa. You are quite happy with it, but it could be a bit more comfortable. Two years later, you are in a furniture store and you see the same model as yours on display. It is identical except it has an extra cushion. All becomes clear. You tell the company that when it delivered the sofa one of the cushions was missing. You expect it to quibble because, after all, it is two years later. But, without hesitation, it agrees to deliver another cushion – and charge you nothing. You are appreciative and delighted.

This is not a pipe dream of customer service. It is based on the real story of a customer of Möbel Kraft in Bad Segeberg. The company knew that believing the customer's word would make him feel positive about the company and get him back in the store.

Consider some examples of the reverse kind of experience. You go into a leading retailer selling bags and luggage to try to get a specific item you have seen in the del Sey catalog. The store does not have what you want in stock. You ask if it can be ordered for you to have a look at. They say no. You politely ask why. The best they can come up with is that: "It will just clutter up our stock room if you don't take it." At 1.00am, you phone a telco to request an alarm call but cannot get through because, according to a recorded message, all lines are busy. You have to wait 10 to 12 weeks for a furniture store to deliver a shelf system assembled from modular parts.

These experiences leave people feeling disappointed, angry, irritated, baffled, mystified. I know: I was that customer! The natural response is to vow that there will never be a next time, that you will go elsewhere, try something else, in future.

Forget about "earnings-oriented management of customer satisfaction." Companies need to get the basics of doing business right.

Providing basics well

If you get the basics right, extras are not necessary. The successful fashion retailer Ipuri is famous for its good service. Its chief executive and owner Edgar Rosenberger once said:

"The best service is the kind which is not felt to be out of the ordinary, but which is simply done."

ALDI's success is based largely on simple and committed customer orientation. I do not remember seeing anyone, in all my years at ALDI, put profits or operational efficiency above the interests of the customer.

When I was general manager in Schleswig-Holstein, Theo Albrecht paid me a visit and, together, we went to one of our stores in Niebüll. Theo Albrecht found a package of three Mars bars (sold for 98 Pf.) torn open on one of the shelves. He took one and went to the cash register. The cashier, understandably excited by the presence of an important visitor, demanded 50 Pf. (one half instead of one third the price of the multipack). When Theo Albrecht showed his surprise she responded by saying: "Mr. Albrecht, when in doubt, we always decide in favor of the company!" She meant well – play it safe! And divide 98 by three under this sort of pressure? He then took time to gently explain what he as a customer might have expected.

Nothing is easier to understand as a value and rule, or more acceptable as a guiding principle, than fair behavior towards the customer. It is simple, sensible and ethical. Clearly and concretely defined service, reliability and credibility are the answers to the buzzwords of consultants and marketing gurus.

Credibility

Credibility is key to good relationships with people – relationships between managers and employees, but also with suppliers and customers. "Credibility is congruence of (consistency in) talking and doing," is how the former head of Nestlé, Helmut Maucher, puts it. ALDI has perfected this idea in relation to its own customers – and they have rewarded the effort.

ALDI adheres to the principle of offering good or even the best quality at the lowest possible price. Customers can trust the offer. They come to know that shopping around for a better price would be pointless. They checked prices against those of competitors at first, but, by now, they know they can relax. The easily manageable, narrow product range allows ALDI managers to keep the relationship between price and value under control.

ALDI has become credible in the eyes of customers because talking and doing, advertising and reality, agree. Customers know their faith is justified because they have never been disappointed. ALDI is something of a customer trustee. It never wants to mislead the customer: what you see is what you get. When the world prices for cocoa rose, one supplier suggested changing the mix of 30 chocolates in the box slightly so that the sales price could be held beneath the "panic threshold" of euro 1.50. ALDI rejected this idea. The price was raised to euro 1.57; that was that.

At a 1996 conference on "Discounting in Germany" sponsored by *Lebensmittel-Zeitung*, ALDI's consistent performance over 30 years was recognized as a factor in its standing with customer and suppliers. The company simply means "reliability" to people. Why else would customers be prepared to buy a "generic" computer at ALDI for euro 1000, without any sales assistance, any recommendation? Only solid trust makes it possible to show a turnover of euro 200m in a matter of three days.

Uncompromising quality and product range policy

For ALDI, good quality is one of the imperatives of close-to-the-customer practice. The company's quality control systems are uncompromising. Long before salmonella hit the headlines, eggs were being tested at ALDI distribution centers by an egg lamp, a simple candling method that checks for freshness. Some other companies do not even know what an egg lamp is. Also, if fast turnover is an additional indicator of freshness, then the freshness of ALDI eggs is assured.

Daily sampling of private label goods, comparing them with leading brands, as well as laboratory tests, complement ALDI's intensive quality policy. This has been true for decades. We did not need "ISO 9000" or "total quality management" (TQM) to make us think it was a good idea.

Quality policy also includes clear and honest presentation of the item. Even at ALDI, however, there are occasional exceptions. We took advantage of the negligible difference between Grand Marnier "Cordon Rouge" and "Cordon Jaune," deciding only to distribute the latter exclusively. "Cordon Jaune," although not markedly different in taste from the cognac, is produced from brandy and is, consequently, much cheaper. While other retailers in Germany sold the much more expensive cognac-based product with the red ribbon we offered an alternative. There was nothing fundamental wrong with the way we presented what we sold. The worst we could be accused of was probably "a sin of omission."

With regard to uncompromising customer orientation, many German retail managers do not follow the principle suggested by Fredmund Malik and implemented by ALDI: the value added per unit, the absolute and percentage gross proceeds, the advertising allowance offered by the supplier should not be the basic decision criteria for deciding on the assortment (see also the section entitled "Success is not decided by purchasing but by the marketing concept"). This is the only way to prevent the supplier filling up your shelves with items which conflict with a sensible, close-to-the-customer sales concept. Discounts in exchange for listing products from suppliers have to be carefully balanced against customer needs.

ALDI's competitors are heavily supplier-oriented, a tendency which often faces major disadvantages which cannot be calculated initially. Uwe Rosmanith refers accurately to the "bias towards purchasing of many companies."[14] In many instances, it is not the items which are purchased but the advertising allowances, refunds and discounts. This practice can be literally "read off the shelves": you will find the same brand of sausages in both 750- and 850-gram jars; customers cannot tell one size from the other, but they fill the store's shelves. The "bias towards purchasing" is increasingly elbowing customer orientation out of day-to-day company management.

Dealing with returns

A company's returns policy is the final test of its commitment to customer service. ALDI was keen to set clear and firm rules that would ensure fair and consistent treatment of customers with grievances. As a principle, ALDI takes back anything that the customer does not like or that is not in perfect condition. Customers are either given a replacement or their money back.

Most companies give the stores some discretion in handling returns to prevent advantage from being taken. ALDI is different. Cases of customers taking advantage of such generosity are extraordinarily rare. Should one arise – the classic scenario involves the bottle that is brought back minus most of its contents – the name and address of the customer is taken down and the case referred to the district manager. The customer is then notified without delay. This procedure is largely intended to eliminate arbitrary behavior by sales assistants.

A report in the *Lebensmittel-Zeitung* of October 4, 1996 gave a perfect illustration of ALDI's policy. It is reproduced below.

Short and sweet at ALDI South

Frankfurt, October 2 – The situation was annoying. But these things happen. The small travel case bought at ALDI South, Wiesbaden in June failed even before the first assignment – the cylinder lock had come out.

Your editor hoped to find a way out of his dilemma by calling the ALDI regional headquarters in Mörfelden. His call was answered by a pleasant and friendly employee who – after hearing the caller's emergency situation – immediately put the call through to a colleague. Ms. T. was also extremely helpful. She suggested the case could be returned at the point of sale and the money refunded. But, she continued, there was also a "service address" that handled cases like this for ALDI. Ms. T looked for the address but could not find it immediately. She called back 20 minutes later and gave me the details: Dario GmbH in Hamburg. At this point, too, the caller, pretty unused to being treated like a king by retailers, detected a polite and conciliatory manner. After an extensive discussion, Ms. R. recommended sending the case to Hamburg; Dario would pay for shipping and handling, and see what could be done.

Despite the tempting offer, your editor took the easy option, and returned the case to ALDI. The reaction that met him at the store in Mainzer Straße in Wiesbaden was initially one of slight surprise, but there was little delay. The manager took the case back even without a receipt. "What did it cost?" she asked. Since she had been on vacation while the special offer was on she was not sure. Your editor – not exactly sure either – said: "29 marks 90, I think." The ALDI employee trusted the customer and paid out the amount.

Service in Germany – it is a joy to be able to report experiences like this!

Obsession with detail: Small triumphs every day

The ALDI concept, with its heavy emphasis on cost consciousness, calls for employees who are interested in practical details – not the vagaries of marketing trends in the year 2010. This interest in details is promoted at ALDI by the complete lack of staff. At ALDI many employees who complete their usual daily tasks as part of the regularly scheduled work are also given additional, interesting assignments, which in other companies would be generally reserved for staff functions. ALDI thus provides "job enrichment," as motivation theorists recommend.

For policies and projects to be implemented successfully, those employees affected must be brought into the development process. There must be involvement at every level of the company hierarchy. This will help pre-empt problems and identify practical solutions. If you have contributions for what you are trying to achieve, the battle is half over. Too many projects fail because they have not been properly thought through, because they meet with resistance from employees and because managers tend to forget that people who do the most menial work can also give an opinion and have ideas. It is the job of management to consult the workforce and then help guide the implementation stage.

The collective knowledge of employees is greater in every company than is generally assumed. To unearth the treasure trove of information, facts, ideas, experiences and insights one needs an organizational framework, a corporate culture, in which employee input is encouraged. A genuine culture of success is one where employees make suggestions on their own initiative and even implement them on their own. Experience is passed on within a company, handed down to new generations of employees. And the success that results from an interest in detail promotes motivation: because success is the greatest motivator.

ALDI thrives on common sense solutions, practical ideas that can be tried out immediately. Management "scientists" or "consultant gurus" are only needed if people are not clear about the company's basic premises or if special questions have to be answered. Common sense professionalism has been at the center of ALDI's cost leadership. With a powerful ability to come up with simple solutions that repeatedly lead to extremely low costs, ALDI is many years ahead of the competition. It has developed what Cuno Pümpin has called "strategic success factors"[15] This ability cannot be developed easily and is impossible to copy.

An utterly uncompromising stand has given ALDI a cost advantage on store rents. Its motto is: a low rent – even in the best of locations – or no rent. It would rather do without a unit than pay a high price for it. Since leases often run for ten years, it was a long time before competitors were able to get anywhere near the top values obtained by ALDI. Some chain stores have rents which amount to 30% of their operating costs. At the new center located in Potsdamer Platz in downtown Berlin ALDI now has a location in the basement. ALDI's rent will be far under that of other tenants, after all ALDI pulls in customers for the others like a magnet, increasing the number of shoppers.

In modern management speak this commitment to continuous improvements in details is known as *kaizen*, at Volkswagen they call the method "CIP²" (continuous improvement process "squared") and VW manager Ignacio Lopez owes his fame to it. What seems to be modern, dressed up in new terminology, is nothing new for ALDI, a firmly established culture which is renewed on a daily basis by setting good examples.

For example, at ALDI the trucks are equipped with tachographs which record the movements of the rear loading gate and allow conclusions to be drawn about productivity and potential unacceptable movements of the loading gate. A study was also made of whether window or lid cut is more advantageous for opening boxes.

Theo Albrecht – store designer

When Theo Albrecht, who would have liked to become an architect, turns his attention to turnstile designs for nearly all the interior plans for new stores – and nearly always find a better solution than the one put forward by the responsible sales manager – it is not just a cost-saving exercise for ALDI . Theo Albrecht also turning his hand to practicalities, because he simply has a "knack" for things like this. Of course, you might ask whether the owner of such a large company has nothing better to do. Whatever the case, Theo Albrecht exemplifies an ALDI characteristic: an attention to details that continuously improves efficiency and productivity. By his example he is indirectly challenging his employees to put more effort into coming up with better solutions. A drawing like this can also result in the regional sales manager's being honored with a phone call from Theo Albrecht: "Put the drawing some-where that you can . . ." and then it is jointly optimized. Success lies in the details.

From Ivory Tower to shop floor

An ALDI general manager knows the details without losing sight of the overall structure. This means in practice that both the members of the administrative board and the general managers show an interest in how fresh the eggs in the stores are. Interest in detail means that even top managers go into the stores, look into every nook and cranny of the company and, pick up on hundreds of opportunities, feed them into the decision-making process, find solutions and implement them – by experimenting, testing, doing.

Managers must be role models; that is one of their main tasks. As member of the administrative board I also made a point of visiting the stores when I carried out control visits to the regional companies. What was important to me was to discreetly observe an employee at his work for a few minutes. I was not so much interested in that particular employee or his level of performance but in simply seeing what the purpose of this specific task was and whether it achieved the desired result effectively and economically. Because there is room for improvement any time, any place. The improvement made in one store can be multiplied by 3,000 stores in Germany. For an assessment of this kind you do not have to be a time and motion specialist – critical, questioning observation suffices.

Leaving the Ivory Tower of the executive suite and descending to the shop floor is often more difficult than philosophizing about grand visions, Marketing 2010 and the fat reports produced by marketing departments and management consultants. Work on the details reveals the daily efforts at the point of sale – a practice which is both necessary and helpful. Less layering and fewer or no staff functions are two ways of fostering this approach. The year 2010 must, of course, be kept in mind, but the actors on the lower levels in particular must be involved in strategy development so that enough attention is paid to the details of daily business and they can be put into proper perspective.

Kajo Neukirchen, one of the masters of corporate reorganization, once said:

"Leading a company means sticking very close to the facts and to operations."

Increasingly, competitors are coming round to the idea that the ALDI way of doing things is the best foundation for long-term success. This is reflected in the fact that they are hiring ALDI staff. Now that business is not as easy as it once was, Norma has recruited the former general managers

Peter Vianden and Harald Scheidenbach as well as the ALDI central purchasers Pierre Schulz and Günther Kujahn to help reshape operations. And Lidl has tried to strengthen its position by bringing in former ALDI South managers, Klaus Gehrig and Werner Hoffmann.

These recruits are certainly making life difficult for their former employer, but simply adding the right people is not enough. There has to be the right framework to support them – the right culture. Norma has become more authoritarian. This is to be regretted: the ability to delegate is, as I will discuss later, one of the prerequisites for success.

An interest in detail or rule crazy?

Of course, attention to detail can have its drawbacks and its dangers. Simplicity can get lost as going deeply into the detail can lead to bureaucracy. Also, as the business gets larger over time and new matters have to be dealt with and rules created, the old ones still remain in force.

At ALDI, however, the risks are relatively small. There are no teams of staff employees dedicated to the production of thick company manuals. For the ALDI line managers, theoretical desk work is always less important than work directly related to practice.

Yet ALDI also has its problems with bureaucracy – at ALDI North under Theo Albrecht more than South under his brother Karl. The reasons for the temporary increase in bureaucracy were mistrust and the composition of the leadership team. In the South there are no general appraisals and no reports about visits by the executives to the stores. ALDI South was always "leaner" than North, where, for example, there are detailed job descriptions and very sophisticated work instructions. At North, for example, at general manager conferences together with the administrative board they devoted time to subjects such as "cleaning the freezers," "letting apartments in company-owned buildings," or "warnings to sales clerks." The "top-level discussions" of the administrative board included "job description for the print shop" as well as "expenses allowed to auditors sent outside of Germany."

A "check list for store managers" consisted of 64 questions, the training plan for cashiers was eight pages long – despite the very simple store organization in comparison to traditional supermarkets. For the sales assistants, the areas of delegation and their tasks were described in great detail, straining the "Harzburg Model," which will be discussed in the second section to the limit. Thirty-six pages were filled with instructions for dealing with inventory loss. The "General Management Guide" was also loaded with too many regulatory details and definitions.

Admittedly, each point taken alone can be justified and, when applied in 3,000 stores, impacts substantially on the business through the multiplier affect. But that is precisely the danger of all bureaucracies. Life also becomes complicated for ALDI employees when they do not keep to the "virtuous path of simplicity." ALDI employees also heavily criticize bureaucratized "guidelines" and many a petty instruction. One of these "guidelines," for example, is a set of desk rules for offices in the stores which states exactly which papers must be kept in which drawers. Refined and highly complicated bonus systems for district managers have also brought more bureaucracy than benefit. Too many bonus factors with innumerable variations lead in the end to confusion and impracticality. Even an information catalog for each supervisory position, a supplement to the job descriptions, can only be viewed as bureaucratic excess. This catalog is supposed to insure that each employee also passes on necessary details to other posts. The "General Management Guide" contains definitions and regulations regarding subjects such as suggestions, instructions, information, workflow, complaints and other matters. Taken separately each is certainly understandable and even sensible, but overall they are more of a burden than a benefit.

Criticism of the bureaucracy comes mostly from the lower end of the organization, from those doing the work, and, in my experience, is justified. The critical point at ALDI was and remains the administrative board, the "highest ranking officers." Here – as in other companies – there are camouflaged power struggles which are reflected in the form and style of instructions.

ALDI's administrative board is like any other, with every member having likes and dislikes about certain methods or ways of behaving. In such situations, everything depends on the person who comes out on top/who manages to assert himself. If the bureaucratic or the doubtful one wins, the corresponding procedures and rules will be put in place. Since the administrative board naturally does not want to debate its differences of opinion in the general manager meeting, it presents a united front there. Then, in general, even good arguments of general managers only have a slight chance of being implemented. This is a growing problem in the ALDI Group that is likely to increasingly hamper the company's performance.

Rigor and system despite daily temptations

Many people – including managers – are fickle in their opinions. The solution seems simple: persistently adhere to clearly identified principles. Resist temptations to change proven methods – remember the adage, "Stick to the knitting." ALDI has nearly always acted on this. Just to name one example: the only product they make is coffee – unlike the Consumer Cooperatives in Germany and A&P in the United States who produced nearly 80% of their products themselves and failed.

Steadfast commitment to principle has, historically, characterized ALDI's operations. The company has resisted temptations to widen the product range, to diversify into other industries, to base purchasing decisions on special deals offered by suppliers. For years, it flatly refused to carry items such as fruit and vegetables, had no telephones in the stores until this became a useful feature with the introduction of IT systems, avoided any form of manipulation in quality, and never took space in high-rent locations. This sort of persistence demands a high degree of discipline and distinguishes the company and its employees.

An example of strong-willed adherence to principles – which at times can border on stubbornness or even blindness – was the way in which butter was treated. Butter was the only important refrigerated product not sold because of fears of massive volumes and that no profit could be expected from the probable sales price. This was in flat contradiction to the much-cited customer orientation. This item was even ruled out in the Netherlands where conditions were totally different. But exceptions (even to intelligent methods) prove the rule and highlight the basically correct thinking. In this case, a lesson could have been learnt from Bismarck, who once said that having principles could on occasion be like running through a forest with a long pole clenched between your teeth. When it came to butter, ALDI had to accept that it had made a mistake.

The increasing competition among discounters is also causing unease in the ALDI organization, which found once it so easy to outmaneuver the competition. So it was no longer possible to simply ignore the potentially interesting sales of butter. On the other hand, refusing to sell butter always had been inconsistent with ALDI's customer orientation. Salt is not an item suitable for a narrow ALDI range either. But salt is sold nevertheless because it is one of the customer's basic needs.

Enormous discipline is required to freeze the number of items for many years. A Nestlé study from 1987 states: "All respondents to a survey of top retail managers agreed that ALDI is moving towards becoming a full-liner." That had actually happened to some competitors. They started as discounters and then widened their product range because they were not sufficiently successful with the original concept. The Swiss discounter Denner went on to expand the number of items on its shelves to 3,000. It is now planning a step-by-step reduction back down to 1,000.

ALDI's commitment to its goals – all of which are underpinned by strict faith in customer orientation – is consistent down to the smallest details. This is why it is different from the opposition. This is why it can boast the famous 1% (profit before taxes as percentage of turnover), which gives its people such a sense of pride, such job satisfaction.

Competitors have failed in copying ALDI largely because they have failed to face up to the contribution made to the company's success by those rare qualities of asceticism, rigor and discipline which many managers find so difficult. They are inclined to miss the "sweet life" of conferences, suppliers' invitations and any interesting distraction of the day. Close attention to detail – rigorously pursued – can only be achieved if people are passionately convinced of the meaning of their work and the success that depends on it. This is true of the majority of ALDI employees. Even most of those employees doing the tougher physical work at the cash registers, in the vehicle fleet or in the distribution centers probably think this way as well. They are not only paid better than any-one else in the industry, they also get a great deal of praise and approval from customers and friends. Nearly everyone praises ALDI for its good performance. And for this, all employees can take credit.

At Ikea, concentration is one of the nine commandments promoted by founder Ingvar Kamprad: "Concentrating our efforts is important for our success. You cannot do everything at the same time."[16] With unflagging persistence, ALDI has concentrated on its traditional business and its clear goals. Peter Drucker once attested:[17]

"Concentration is the key to business results. No other principle of effectiveness is infringed today on such a regular basis as the basic principle of concentration. Our motto seems to be: let us do a little bit of everything."

"Management by mistrust"?

In 1992, the German business weekly *Wirtschaftswoche* described the system run by ALDI's "buttoned-lips" as "management by mistrust." Was this a fair assessment? With a few exceptions relating more to the owners, no. It is probably universally acknowledged that owners tend to be mistrustful – after all, their money is at stake. It is equally true that Theo Albrecht's mistrust influenced the control culture in the company. But the management practised using ALDI's control systems can be considered a model for many other companies.

Nobody should be afraid of thinking about the rights and wrongs of control processes, from a quite unbiased standpoint. Egon Zehnder from the consultancy Zehnder International considers Lenin's remark, "Confidence is good, control is better," to be dumb and damaging. He is right; I completely agree. But might there not be some circumstances when control is acceptable – or even essential?

Many companies could do with taking the issue of control more seriously and tackling it more professionally. When the German public prosecutor's office was investigating the background to the bankruptcy of Bremer Vulkan AG, statements made by the former board member, Manfred Timmermann, hardly reflected well on the supervisory board. "The CEO was able to call the shots without interference, the supervisory board rubber stamped everything. With better management, the impending financial collapse at what was once Germany's largest shipbuilding consortium could have been prevented."

The supervisory board is responsible for ensuring good management at the top of a company. The board can only discharge its duties if it has an adequate system of control: it is not enough to rely on the reports of auditors and to believe the word of the directors it is there to supervise. The ALDI administrative board observes a highly-disciplined, serious control system – a system practiced throughout all levels of the hierarchy.

The system is based on spot checks that each supervisor applies to his employees every month. In my opinion, checks should be made on all employees who are given decision-making responsibilities. Indeed, these employees have a right to it. To monitor people is to recognize their achievements. Employees should never be given tasks and responsibilities if they are not considered capable or trustworthy enough to carry them out. Trust is the basic prerequisite for delegation. Nevertheless, it is important for supervisors to check whether and how the delegated tasks are being carried out. This can eliminate misunderstandings that may have arisen when the task was assigned. Through the control procedure, both partners have the opportunity to discuss their expectations. Control is intended to eliminate sources of errors and reduce the risk to the company. Lack of control explains why, for example, the discounter

Penny (Rewe Group) shows less profit than ALDI. The store inventories are probably at least 1% poorer. This would cost ALDI euro 150m annually.

The "supervision [of work] in the context of delegation" developed by Professor Reinhard Höhn at the Business Management Academy in Bad Harzburg has had an impact on ALDI's day-to-day business. The control procedures practised at ALDI can be referred to as system-defining and system-supporting and have contributed to the company's success. Like obsession with detail and a rigorous approach and correctness and, finally, the principle of delegation, they have become an integral part of the corporate culture.

Experiment instead of endless analysis

In their book *In Search of Excellence*, Peters and Waterman promote the KISS approach – "Keep It Simple, Stupid!" The acronym could have been invented with ALDI in mind. ALDI people are doers. Everything is tried out, as fast as possible; they don't get tied down in endless, in-depth analyses. There could hardly a better driver of the innovation so frequently lacking in business than opening up the opportunity to invent and try out absolutely everything that could serve the company's objectives. Another favorable point at ALDI is that by experimenting you cannot upset someone else's agenda. There are no staff functions to complain about possible infringement of their territory.

A telling example, and one which had consequences for the ALDI Group as a whole, was provided by the colleagues in Holland. Until about 1985, the ALDI cashiers always had to memorize the sales prices of all 600 items so that the goods did not have to be price-labeled. The disadvantage of this was that when prices changed they had to memorize the changes as well. When a cashier came back to work from vacation they had to learn more new ones than usual.

One solution might have been item numbers which could be memorized for each item and which could be identified by the data cash registers similar to scanner systems. For many years, ALDI management considered this solution to be too difficult and impossible to implement. They assumed that cashiers could remember "talking" prices much better, and assumed that the price – for example for a kilo of sugar set at euro 0.85 contained a certain statement and was something like a recognizable unit – simply because of its amount. In retrospect, this was a gullible, naive assumption, since it was never proven.

At the ALDI company in Ommen, Overijssel, under their director A. D. Conijn, the Dutch simply tried out the new method typing item numbers instead of prices "in secret." Finally they introduced their German colleagues to this innovation which to date has resulted in the fastest and cheapest data cash register in the world at ALDI North. No scanner register can deliver such quick register performance, and not in such an uncomplicated and inexpensive way.

Given that, like Einstein, the Albrechts preferred to "grope their way forward," it is no surprise that ALDI operates completely without consultants – there are no management consultants, no market researchers, no advertising consultants. Only in extremis does the company engage external legal advisers. And even then it proceeds with caution – no legal advice is acted on unless it has been intensively discussed and dissected. The ALDI people are so interested in details that they want to understand for themselves what is at stake and what the law says.

The secret, or the art of simplicity

As I have said, ALDI's success story is a lesson in simplicity. Although customer orientation, asceticism, rigor and discipline are essential ALDI features, simplicity is the company's real secret.

ALDI is a master of the art of implementing what is thought of as "expected, normal and reasonable." There is only one way – a "culture of simplicity." In this, the company has much in common with Ikea, whose founder, Ingvar Kamprad, describes simplicity as a virtue: *"Complex rules hamper companies, excessive planning is the most common cause of corporate death. Simplicity fortifies."*[18]

It is incredibly difficult to be simple. Perhaps such behavioral models and cultures are typical for companies oriented to a single person, family operations which have been influenced for a long time by the owner. The essential quality of the owner as a chief executive is that he is not under contract to work for a limited period and will not leave the company again after several months or years, leaving his post to a successor, who will attempt to introduce a new culture. Developing a corporate culture takes time.

Owner operated companies generally start small and take many years to mature. A culture which is largely determined by an owner cannot be easily copied.

When I became general manager of the ALDI site in Nortorf, my former boss, Horst Langenbucher, director of coop Schleswig-Holstein, asked if he could visit our new distribution center. I refused. I did not want to contravene the ALDI rule of confidentiality, for one thing, but the main reason was that I did not want anyone to see how simply we practiced the so-called "science of logistics." Then, as now, the ALDI organization was reputed to have many secrets. I had no wish to disabuse the minds of the competition.

Of course, I am not trying to imply that ALDI is unique. This is how the Scania organization explains its consistently high performance, relative to competitors, in the global truck market. "There is very little which Scania does much better than competitors. Except for one thing: the Swedes rigorously pursue the principle of simplicity. Simple designs, simple production processes, simple product pallets, and simple management structures."

They could easily have been talking about ALDI. Many computer software users also complain about a lack of simplicity. Perhaps Microsoft and others should think a little bit about whether a "discount windows," freed of a lot of ballast, wouldn't make life easier for a lot of people.

Dell Computer Corporation works on ALDI-like principles: clear targets, avoidance of distractions, concentration on a few basics. Dell's clean-cut corporate targets have made it strong. It is the biggest in its field but has only half the costs of its competitors.

Procter & Gamble also likes simple ways of doing things. "Make it simple" is quoted by *Business Week* as the group's guiding corporate principle. P&G points out that often only one unit per month is sold of around a quarter of all the items stocked by large supermarkets. Insights like this – long-accepted facts of retailing – urgently call for new ways of thinking.

Carrying a product range of, say, 20,000 or more items has implications for every operational rung of an organization. It makes managing companies and their processes difficult. Even the small supermarkets, including small Edeka outlets, sometimes sell more than 30 kinds of roasted coffee, 40 kinds of sausages in cans and jars. In Malaysia, I have seen super-markets with 120 kinds of powdered milk – the same product from different makers, a huge number of brands, various sizes, various packages, slightly different tastes. A small store can sell Omo detergent in packages of 800, 1,300, 2,500, 3,000, 4,500 and 8,000 grams and – just for good measure – carry equivalents from two or three competing brands.

The orientation to suppliers instead of customers plus these unnecessary duplications leads to the vast number of items in the store, which make the management of the companies and all processes complicated.

So what does ALDI's principle of simplicity mean in practice? To answer this question, it is important to understand that simplicity and thoroughness are not mutually exclusive. ALDI's simple solutions, founded on basic ideas, basic principles, are supported by carefully planned practical arrangements.

Characteristics of the ALDI simplicity are listed below.

- No large central functions such as marketing, management accounting, information systems, public relations, advertising, legal department; no staff functions.
- Clear targets and responsibilities for everyone that are strictly adhered to.
- A flat structure run on the principles of decentralization and delegation.
- Few statistics are recorded; regular surveys and analyses of data – such as average customer purchases – are studiously avoided.
- No complex purchasing conditions.
- Few direct suppliers to the stores (e.g., one supplier each for baked goods and frozen foods).
- New products are piloted in three stores. This avoids burdening the whole organization with a possible flop.
- Making sales directly out of delivery boxes.
- Taking deliveries exclusively on pallets.
- Placing goods in the store to meet logistical needs, make work easier and increase productivity. No attempt is made to place at "eye level" those goods on which the profit margin is higher.
- Use of a simple cash register system, without scanners.

One of the greatest virtues of simplicity is that it speeds things up. Time is the most precious resource. Make life too complicated and you may achieve nothing. The connection between time and simplicity becomes very apparent from the ideas of the neurobiologist Christof Koch at CalTech California. He discussed his research in the field of consciousness theory with the German weekly newspaper Die Zeit (July 2, 1998). Various experts were accusing him of limiting his analysis exclusively to the visual system. How could he be so sure that he could succeed? His answer is a description of the principle of success simplicity: "I don't think it's possible at present to develop a theory of consciousness which is compatible with all our insights. Our knowledge of the brain is too fragmentary. So one has to decide for one approach and pursue it without letting oneself be driven completely off course by inconsistent results. It is quite simple: I want to understand the problem in my lifetime. Of course one has to explain at some time the various states of consciousness. But if you have lost your house key, you look for the simplest way of entering your house – and, at present, that is conscious and unconscious sight. Of course, it may be that the only door which is open merely leads to the storage room."

ALDI has become a success by doing without many alternative routes, by concentrating on one approach, by trial and error. ALDI 's approach is similar to that of Christof Koch.

The question "Why?"

The principles of simplicity often underlie efforts to make companies "lean" – i.e., manageable, clear, comprehensible, reasonable, intelligent. The simple solutions deliver success. Companies need to ask the kind of simple questions that children do.

In his book, *The Secret of Toyota's Production Success*, Shigeo Shingo describes the significance of the "W questions." But he is not talking about "what," "when," "why," "who" and "where." The five Ws at Toyota are: "Why?" "Why?" "Why?" "Why?" and "Why?"

Asking "why?" clears things up. The more frequently the question why is asked – particularly in the context of business and political processes – the question about the sense and purpose of things, measures and ideas, the clearer and simpler the answers become. Another great, new statistic! Why? Try the following experiment in your own corporate environment: approach the author of the latest paper creations, or those who ordered their creation, and throw questions at them. You'll be amazed. Companies often attribute too much importance to the question of "how?" which is the domain of the technocrats and engineers. While asking "how?" remains an important question, it should follow rather than lead; the purpose, or "Why?" should take precedence. This is also applicable in the simplest of instances, one example being the question "Why should we put this item on our conference agenda?"

The success of ALDI is inseparably linked to the simple design of systems and processes. The path of "fanatic simplicity" is always the more intelligent one. Companies must attempt to come to grips with the complexities of the world by simplifying their organizational processes. **Intelligent design is simple design.**

The companies that survive in an increasingly competitive environment will be those whose mastery of complexity is clearly and simply organized. The computer manufacturer Compaq could well be one of these structures; in its ads, Compaq writes that it is looking for "simple solutions to complex tasks."

A word regarding the necessity of budgets is appropriate at this point. There is hardly a manager or corporate executive today who can imagine working without annual or departmental budgets. Come September, budget preparations and budget negotiations begin, requiring an infinite number of costly management working hours and causing frustration amongst staff at every level of the company. Yet, budgets and forecasts are not necessary. ALDI has proven it.

Shrewd self-restraint on product mix

One of the decisive factors behind this simplicity is without a doubt ALDI's product mix, which was limited to 600 items for several decades.

ALDI's simplicity, achieved by means of a limited number of items, was not solely the consequence of extraordinary intelligence, but also the result of Karl Albrecht's experiences, documented in 1953 and then vigorously pursued over the years.

In many industries, people have come to recognize that variety is a substantial cost factor. The automotive industry was one of the main ones to grapple intensively with this problem, as reports about the variety of parts at Volkswagen show. As the number of variants or items in a product range grows, so too does the level of cost and complexity. Empirically quantified findings about the relationships between cost and the number of items offered in retailing are not, to the author's knowledge, actually available; however, a graph of the reality in retail outlets would probably produce the following curve.

The complexity curve

Costs
Complexity
Organizational rigidity

"The mysterious rise in costs"

Number of items (or components/subassemblies/rules and laws)

According to Christian Homburg, professor of business economics at the Business Management School in Koblenz,[19] infrastructural overhead costs rise very much in proportion to the number of variants. Frequently, too many variants are produced as a result of lack of information. Managers make the mistake of thinking that the new variant can be handled within the existing infrastructure – i.e., without raising the fixed costs of doing business.

Creeping cost growth can be the result. While not visible at first, costs will later be seen to have increased – for no apparent reason. The fact that each additional item influences the already existing mix may be adequately recognized, but there is a lack of rigor in turning this knowledge into action, without bias or illusions. Often, the sales function will demand an expansion of the mix with the argument that "this would be in the customer's interests." Purchasing is also aware of these apparent "needs" as a result of discussions with suppliers who have once again thought up a new discount or creative incentive for adding another item; even industry advertising contributes to dangerous product mix expansions: whatever you do, don't let anything slip through your fingers, don't let good opportunities pass you by, don't mess up, don't miss a single deal. The fact of the matter however, is that these "necessities" are frequently non-existent. Handling this dilemma need not require perplexing, new and complex "complexity management." Rather, it just requires simple and shrewd organization.

A very convincing example of this approach is supplied by a relatively new discounter in another country which began by frenetically experimenting with its mix, but which can be used to provide a nice demonstration of the principles of discounting and simplicity.

Product range and turnover history for detergents use in washing machines

Item	Turnover 1996 Nov	Turnover 1996 Dec	Turnover 1997 Mar	Turnover 1997 May	Possible correct policy
Omomatik – 3,000g	44,000	56,800	2,000*		60,000
Omomatik – 2,000g			26,500	23,500	
Omomatik – 4,000g				27,000	
Omomatik – 4,500g			37,950	1,000*	
Omomatik – 1,300g	7,150	13,250	4,300	4,500*	15,000
Omomatik – 800g			9,500	11,000	
Rinsomatik – 3,000g	39,050	41,950	33,800	31,500	40,000
Bingomatik – 3,000g	9,450*				
Allmatik† – 3,000g	18,000	25,800	20,350	24,000	30,000
Total	117,650	137,800	134,400	122,500	145,000

* Each cancelled item   † Private label

If the principles of "concentration" had been observed in every way (right column), the result would have been a clearer policy vis-à-vis customers. The company could have considerably strengthened its purchasing power with regards to individual suppliers; unease, confusion and tumult could have been avoided had the company tested new ideas in a few stores rather than have the entire organization be burdened by repeated forward charges and retreats.

A source of error: Cost accounting

Poor cost accounting is one of the enemies of simplicity. It prevents the design of systems that give a clear basis for decisions. Antiquated systems are still being used instead of modern methods such as marginal cost accounting. ALDI does not have any of that

The vehicle fleet manager and his general manager have to maximize productivity and reduce the costs of the vehicle fleet. The implications of that for the customers to be supplied, and the individual stores, is duly considered. But that does not mean that everything has to be confused and the costs of the fleet distributed amongst all the stores using supposedly scientific methods and dubious causality theories. It is quite enough to know the vehicle fleet costs, how they relate to other factors and what determines them.

In the October 1991 issue of *manager magazin*, McKinsey consultant Michael Roever discussed three illusions regarding the subject of costs and complexity which are compared below with ALDI practices.

The first illusion: "If the market stagnates and players are trying to force each other out of the market, the right sales tool is to expand the product range to include niche customers (Complexity I). Despite stagnation and aggressive competition, ALDI has not widened its product range for decades or sought niche customers. Historically, the range has been changed according to the criterion of customer interest. However, that is now changing, as I will discuss in the Outlook chapter.

The second illusion: "We are a major customer; on our order lists there is an enormous volume of semi-finished products and services. We would benefit by adding steps to our value chain to capture our suppliers' profits and obtain other advantages such as greater customer loyalty, quality and improved secrecy" (Complexity II). ALDI follows the simple principle: "Stick to the knitting." ALDI does without any private production (with the exception of roasted coffee). There is no import company, no representative in Hong Kong. But ALDI works with agencies who, of course, take their share of the retail margin for their work and thus, at first sight, theoretically narrow ALDI's profit margin.

The third illusion: "We can really exploit our size if we pull together the functions which can be found in many of our businesses or even in all of them to form central functions, we can benefit from economies of scale and a high degree of functional professionalism" (Complexity III). The ALDI organization is a model of decentralization. Only central cash management, purchasing and "a little bit" of data processing are brought together in centralized functions. ALDI has learnt by experience that it is not centralizing functions that cuts costs, but breaking them up! Moreover, "professionalism" sounds like a dubious term in a number of ways.

Roever describes the fatal path of the so-called synergies that bring complexity and costs in their train and nearly always remain an illusion. So how important is it to introduce improvements in daily routine? Kaizen is one answer to this.

The fear of making mistakes

Decentralization and delegation are two of the key tenets of ALDI simplicity. Large size and growth automatically create complexity at first.

The response of employees and managers is usually to set up complex systems and structures, to establish central staff functions. This is a critical error. It is much more important to maintain the functionality of the whole of the organization and the whole of the company. Primarily, that means making facts and processes clear to the thousands of people at the frontline – the employees. They are the real "doers" in any company. This clarity arises when you express yourself simply, and organize for transparency, manageability, simplicity.

Decentralization and delegation aimed at achieving simple structures means keeping job specifications and "management by objectives" to an absolute minimum. An employee's own judgment should be trusted above a rigid set of rules.

Fear of making mistakes, of being unable to justify something to the supervisory board or to shareholders, often lies at the root of overcomplexity. This fear is undoubtedly more wide-spread in stock companies than in owner-managed ones. Management seeks refuge in complicated systems, in staff departments, in the views of management consultancies. Fear is the cradle of bureaucracy.

Generally accepted guidelines and principles should take the place of detailed individual instructions and of precise rules and regulations governing departmental policies and work practices. But for this to happen, clarity and the question "why" have to become the yardsticks by which actions and decisions are measured. Bureaucracy slows a company down and increases its costs.

The trial and error approached favored by ALDI requires courage. Provided, however, the right questions about a decision have been asked – "Why are we doing this? – there is little reason to worry. And the question as to whether all the bits and pieces envisaged for a solution or process are actually needed, or whether anything could be left out, will automatically follow.

ALDI's approach, then, is minimalistic. Its processes are finely-honed, as simple as possible.

"Great art has been achieved when nothing more can be left out."
Chinese proverb

What is special about ALDI's corporate culture?

ALDI is a role model for the development of discount concepts all over the world – Japan, the United States, Asia, Europe. But what is especially characteristic of the ALDI success story? Its achievements do not stem from substantial windfall profits, or depend on a single, fantastic invention or a patent. Is Daimler-Benz a success story? With the exception of a few years around 1990 and the early problems with the A-Class, and nowadays with Chrysler, no doubt it is. And Tengelmann's profit of 1% of turnover from so many different businesses? There are presumably very few people at Tengelmann who know where the profits are really coming from or what is contributing to losses.

ALDI's qualities are those attributed by Don Clifford and Richard E. Cavanagh to successful mid-sized companies in the United States.[20] Their findings are similar to those of Peters and Waterman. According to them, successful companies are characterized by:

- strong sense of mission (passionately pursued values and goals)
- unlimited attention to fundamental, business tasks
- fierce opposition to any bureaucracy combined with an eagerness to experiment
- an ability to think like the customer.

But in addition to these factors, ALDI has something else. Rolf Berth has examined "uniqueness" as a competitive factor in great detail. According to him, companies like Ikea, ALDI, Swatch and Benetton have something unique about them. For ALDI, it is probably its above-average rigor. "ALDI was and remains the sole discounter that firmly maintains its sales strategy without falling for the temptation of going upmarket," says Berth.

To be unique, you have, says Berth, to have a "measure of madness and abnormality" which makes imitation hard. There is, though, method in ALDI's madness.

The special characteristics of the ALDI corporate culture can be summarized as:

Asceticism and low profile
There is no place – anywhere in the hierarchy – for personal vanity.
Extreme frugality is a must. Waste is prohibited.

Total customer orientation
Earning the trust of the customer means no tricks or sales ploys.

Devotion to and a passion for detail
Small wins count. The aim should be to achieve them daily.

Simple systems
Implement the principle of simplicity and develop the courage to go for simple and rapid solutions.

Rigor in action
Resist daily temptations and stick steadfastly to good concepts.

Part 2
Organization and leadership

Good organization compensates for poor leadership

"A company's success or failure is not determined by good or bad luck, but by how it is led."

This point made by Konosuke Matsushita, founder of Panasonic and one of the world's most successful entrepreneurs, has stayed with me ever since I experienced the deep truth contained in it at ALDI. A good business idea is essential. But nearly everything that follows has to do entirely with company management, leadership, organization, and corporate culture.

If Matsushita's statement is valid, it makes clear the sort of responsibility which leadership personalities bear. In the course of my consulting work and during my years as a manager this truth was to be confirmed over and over again. I developed the chart below which shows how leadership and organization inter-relate.

A company's resources (hardware and software) are the raw materials of its success. They are combined by the organization and the leadership qualities within the company, and directed into the right channel. Organization and leadership qualities can make this channel broad or narrow, restricting or facilitating the flow. The results will differ accordingly. Even poor resources can lead to good results given capable leadership and organization. By contrast, plentiful resources can be throttled by poor leadership and organization, producing mediocre results. Good organization can compensate for poor leadership, and superior leadership for defective organization. Good organization and leadership can improve a company's software, in particular. But shortcomings are frequently to be found in leadership.

Leadership and organization determine success

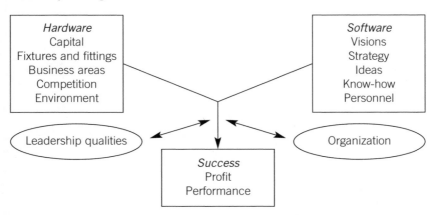

It may offer some consolation and support to company owners and members of supervisory boards (i.e. those in charge of keeping the management on track) to know that they can compensate for these shortcomings by intelligent – including person-related – organization. But they need courage and determination to implement such structures.

A good organization compels a less than ideal leadership to act within a specific framework at least to acceptable standards, even if only for a transitional period. Leadership errors cannot be spotted before they happen, and they can happen anytime. But the organization can be designed right up front, and new managers will adapt to it. If good managers are available, the organization can also be adapted to the employees.

For example, certain managers can be assigned more duties and responsibilities than their official roles call for. There is no need to stick to a predetermined job description. Of course, such flexible methods are easier to apply if you are managing a small company or if a large company can be organized into smaller units with a high degree of autonomy. At ALDI, this is only possible to a limited extent, since the intention is to give the regional companies and their managers identical duties and responsibilities. But potential leadership weaknesses at ALDI are certainly compensated for by its solid organization based on the principles of delegation and decentralization.

Only a minimum of communication

Organizations should always be simply designed and easy to understand, featuring flat hierarchies and simple business procedures. This results in minimized cost structures and coordination effort, and requires only a minimum of necessary communication between the members of the organization.

> *"The purpose of organization is to reduce the amount of communication and coordination necessary. Hence organization is a radical attack on communication problems."*
> Frederick P. Brooks Jr.

Frederick P. Brooks Jr. was the project manager at IBM responsible for the legendary IBM/360 that was introduced in 1964. Ten thousand employees had spent several years working on this enormous project which for decades was considered industry standard throughout the world, ranking with the invention of byte architecture marked the end of the pioneering era in information technology.

This system has been described as one of the largest private development projects in industrial history.

In his book *The Mythical Man-Month*, Brooks describes his experiences and a number of basic insights, among them the above quoted sentence. According to his theory, as many small units as possible should be created within a company or a project in such a manner that these units can basically work independently of each other. This avoids unnecessary running around, costs, and friction and accelerates projects. The question of the speed of projects and how to improve it is also largely a question of good organization. It is often less important how many employees and how much capital is put into a project. In the course of the project Brooks also discovered that programming work cannot simply be accelerated by putting more programmers on it. Often, only a limited number of people can work on a single task, just as a nine-month pregnancy cannot be shortened by putting two women on the job.

But in most companies little attention is paid to Brooks' maxims. General opinion holds communication to be especially important. In many cases that is undoubtedly true, for example where communication between a supervisor and his employees is concerned. And coordination is also needed between departments. But according to Brooks' experience, decreasing the amount of coordination and communication between the various levels of the company should be a primary goal

Most retail organizations typically have strictly separate purchasing and sales functions. Purchasing managers generally determine the product ranges and are expected to adhere to costing specifications. However, since market demand influences choices involving product range and prices, companies set up coordination teams made up of staff from purchasing and sales who meet, for example, once a week for a marketing discussion during which intensive and time-consuming communication and necessary coordination take place.

It does not have to be done this way. ALDI also separates purchasing and sales but, thanks to a manageable product range of 700 items, ALDI's overall situation is fundamentally different. The management decides on assortments and prices based in principle solely on sales considerations. Purchasing, on the other hand, has the clearly defined task of obtaining the defined goods at the lowest possible price from reliable suppliers. How to achieve this goal in practice is basically left entirely to the discretion of the purchasing function. This system requires very little in the way of coordination and communication.

Thus ALDI has been able to avoid setting up costly overhead and staff functions that are associated with high general administration costs and coordination requirements. Many companies are asking themselves today very seriously what staff department X is really needed or useful for and whether the company's goals could not be achieved less expensively without it. This is one of the reasons for the currently observable rapid dismantling of hierarchies which is frequently linked to harsh consequences, especially in middle management. Why are large planning departments and systems necessary and useful? Perhaps they are more suitable for supplying supervisors and supervisory bodies with information and an excuse for their own existence instead of meeting customer needs.

Other companies have now also recognized this issue after decades of friction losses and invented "category management," an approach which is correct in principle but which, however, is yet another complex artifice with its own snags. Questions related to category management are addressed in detail in the section entitled "Success is not decided by purchasing but by the marketing concept."

In manufacturing, comparable areas of conflict can be seen between marketing and sales. Here, too, companies should think more about merging tasks. The divisions of labor promoted by Taylorism are vanishing, why should they be preserved in such intimately related fields as marketing and sales? This is tearing a single whole apart to throw the pieces to two separate departments.

The German company with the best organization

In June 2000, the reputable business magazine Wirtschaftswoche published the results of an image survey. Three thousand four hundred German directors, general managers and managers were polled. "Which is the most innovative major company in Germany?" The survey sought the personal opinion of top managers in Germany. The ten biggest-selling companies from each of 16 industries were included. The evaluated categories were: product and service performance, organization, market visibility, leadership and corporate culture and, finally, the innovation image of the individual companies. Innovation was defined as: new, promising, dynamic, growth promoting.

This is the ranking of the first 10 companies out of a total of 160 global companies operating in Germany:

Overall innovation image	Company	Innovation image evaluation (1 is best)	Product and service performance	Organization	Market visibility	Leadership culture
1	DaimlerChrysler	1.85	1	25	3	10
2	Hugo Boss	1.96	2	7	2	9
3	SAP	1.98	3	5	8	1
4	Bertelsmann	2.04	6	3	18	3
5	Hewlett-Packard	2.05	12	4	12	2
6	Nestlé	2.06	7	8	6	7
7	Otto Versand	2.08	16	2	10	4
8	Coca-Cola	2.08	31	9	1	8
9	**ALDI**	**2.09**	**5**	**1**	**16**	**36**
10	Heidelberger Druck	2.11	3	5	19	5

ALDI's No. 1 ranking in organization ahead of such important companies as Lufthansa, Siemens, BMW, IBM, Compaq, Procter & Gamble, Volkswagen, Philip Morris, Shell, Esso, Unilever, Deutsche Bank and ABB is really something admirable. However, ALDI's position at No. 36 in leadership and culture, which I consider its real success factor, is underestimated by managers because they have only a little insight into the company (remember "What is essential is invisible to the eye.")

The organization of an ALDI company

The ALDI organization is flat, simple, lean. In the operating units, too, there are only line functions with clear responsibilities and levels of authority that are defined in job descriptions. Teams that are only authorized to make good recommendations do not exist at ALDI, as is shown by the following overview.

Organization of an ALDI company (legal form GmbH & Co. KG)

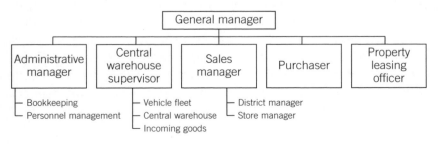

Each ALDI company can have one or two sales managers. Each sales manager is in charge of four to six district managers, each district manager being responsible for seven to ten stores. Each ALDI company operates approximately 40 to 80 stores. When they become large enough to require two sales managers, a kind of cell division generally takes place. Prior to the cell division it is not unusual for there to be up to 100 stores in the old company, and a new company, immediately after the cell division, can consist of as few as 25 stores.

The administrative manager is of course responsible for administrative duties, including the personnel department and electronic data processing. However, the personnel department at ALDI has no authority over the employees. Its responsibilities are purely administrative. The responsibilities of the administrative manager also include coordination with the Works Council and advising and representing the company in matters involving labor law.

The sales manager manages all the stores through the district managers. A person in this position is specifically responsible for ensuring that the stores operate smoothly and cost-efficiently.

The manager of the central warehouse controls the flow of merchandise from when they are received until when they are supplied to the stores. This includes storage handling and fleet management.

The purchaser is essentially responsible for the right inventory levels and reordering from suppliers. He carries out quality assurance and looks for new items for the product range by studying the market and the competition. Moreover, he manages special regional range allowed to each ALDI company: the companies are allowed to make independent decisions on some 30 items not carried by ALDI as a whole. Such products are frequently later introduced into the basic assortment as a result.

The property manager looks for new locations and signs and manages property lease agreements.

An essential role in the ALDI organization is assumed by the central purchasing company, ALDI Einkauf GmbH & Co. OHG. It is a subsidiary of the regional ALDI companies. It negotiates with suppliers and buys all the merchandise. For ALDI North, for example, only six purchasers handle all procurement work: analysis of the supply markets, finding suppliers, quality assessments, negotiations on prices and terms and conditions, signing contracts. Alongside this, the Einkauf OHG handles some services such as centralized cash management, statistical operating comparisons and IT tasks.

The general manager conference: Authoritarian tendencies on the increase

The main decision-making body for basic organizational, policy-making, and conceptual questions is the general manager conference which meets regularly and in which all the general managers of the regional ALDI companies together with the administrative board participate. The general manager conference is the institution that holds ALDI together. Product range and price policies in particular are discussed by the conference in great detail and approved jointly. Final decisions do not require unanimity, but in most cases members of the meeting can support the results of intensive debate.

The consensus-based or majority-rule approach practised in many companies is unknown at ALDI. At ALDI consensus decision making is extremely rare. There are no ballots with decisions based on a majority of votes. Correspondingly, there are few compromises. Compromises are nearly always sub-optimal, so discussions continue until a best solution is found. The issues are discussed thoroughly. It is generally known what sort of strange forms the consensus-based approach can take in politics. Too often groups and parties are all too ready to reach a compromise, so that they can be done with the subject and, at the same time, avoid a really major conflict as far as possible. But in these cases valuable time is generally wasted in any case in the preparations and analyses. You have to get down to the roots of a conflict and, to this end, radical approaches are helpful.

Hans-Olaf Henkel, the former President of the Bundesband der Deutschen Industrie (Federal Association of German Industry), rightly demands an "end to the consensus sauce."[21] Consensus can be dangerous in large businesses as well as in government, if for no other reason than that the best options are often not chosen.

The ALDI general managers prepare themselves very carefully for these discussions at their own companies. They usually hold long discussions about the coming agenda with their management teams. Usually the topics for discussion are raised by the general managers or come from their companies. The discussions are chaired by members of the administrative board. For several years now these members have been increasingly inclined to tip the scale when opinions differ. At ALDI, the practice of discussing topics in breadth and depth until the widest possible agreement is reached is going out of fashion. Authoritarian tendencies are gaining ascendancy. The proven system of delegation and personal autonomy of the employees in the regional business only resumes when the conference is over.

Despite these – possibly temporary – changes in the management culture, I consider that there is no room for the democratic principles of majority decisions in business management. The goal must be to achieve the best results, and the decisive factor here is how the discussions are approached. Finally, everyone involved must be clear about the fact that there are no real and absolute truths, so that agreeing to other people's suggestions cannot be difficult.

The foundations of good leadership and organization

During my years at ALDI I learnt what the foundations of good organization and leadership are. They can be described very simply:

- clear goals,
- few but easily understandable business principles,
- total customer orientation,
- uncompromising thoroughness in the application and implementation of concepts, and
- attention to detail at all levels.

A good organization, guided by these principles, prevents fevered action for action's sake that can often lead to crises. Employees, given their own responsibility, perform their jobs as important cogs in the wheel. There is no room for an all-powerful, hectic boss who just pushes the tiller hard across and changes tack for the sake of it. Who says his gut-feel is reliable?

The leadership and organizational principles at ALDI suited me down to the ground. This was probably why I not only learnt a great deal at ALDI, especially during my ten years as a member of the administrative board, I also was able to contribute substantially to the company's success. In recognition of this, Theo Albrecht informed me of my appointment to the Board of the Theo Albrecht Trust (in the washroom – he was not a man for ceremony).

Clear goals prevent conflict

In many companies objectives, approaches, and methods of all sorts are kept so ambiguous or even secret that ceaseless skirmishes and stand-offs of varying disruptive intensity are staged over truths, apparent truths, and personal opinions. Frequently these disagreements penetrate right through to the supervisory bodies, where interest groups are also formed.

A company like ALDI, led by clear goals and rules, creates an atmosphere in which what has to be said, can be said openly by any employee. Tricks or tedious efforts at persuasion are not necessary.

ALDI's clear business concept, supported by its decentralized organizational structure, helps to reduce the potential for conflict. Of course this does not rule out the possibility of individuals with their idiosyncrasies disrupting the atmosphere and spirit of cooperation, and there are tangible differences between different ALDI companies, depending on their general managers and management teams. But their potential influence – overall – is quite limited.

The targets set at ALDI are extraordinarily simple. The only concern is lowest costs, or rather maximum performance and productivity in all areas, lowest possible sales prices and best quality. This is understood by every cashier, and by every packer in the warehouse. These are goals that can be applied and implemented in all departments by any employees on an ongoing basis. Differentiating between short, medium and long-term goals is unnecessary, nor is there any need for a hierarchy of objectives from the top executives to the lowest ranking employees in the stores. Employees on all levels, whatever their functions, wherever they may be, can use the same goals for orientation: strategies, plans, and goals are not the secrets of the "palace guard," they are known throughout the company.

What ALDI wants is understandable to anyone: not a single cent must be wasted. Every employee can be proud if he succeeds in contributing to the implementation of this goal in his own sphere, even if his area of responsibility is limited. This requires daily detailed work, daily rethinking, daily improvements and exchanges of experience to reach the overall optimum or, initially, the rock-bottom minimum cost.

The unwritten corporate goal is described in concrete terms in the job descriptions for the individual departments.

General managers:
- Must achieve the highest possible turnover on a long-term basis and strengthen the company's market position by expanding and securing a high-performance chain of stores.
- Clear the best profits possible without endangering the company's future development.

- Apply the principle of economy in extreme form to consolidate and expand the company's market position.

Sales managers:

- Must ensure that, in their sales area, the highest possible turnover is achieved on a permanent basis.
- The above requires them to ensure that business runs smoothly in tidy stores at the lowest possible costs whilst delivering the highest possible performance and accurate accounts, in order to maintain and improve the company's competitiveness.
- They must staff the stores with managers who meet the demands of the position and ensure that their district managers perform their duties in compliance with the job descriptions.

The district managers:

- Must put the right staff in place in the stores to keep them clean and tidy, ensure a smooth sales process and correct inventories, and achieve high sales.
- Must ensure that the instructions issued by management are carried out in the same way in all stores.

The store managers:

- Are responsible for keeping their stores clean and tidy at all times.
- Ensure adequate supplies of merchandise (avoiding both surplus stock and short-falls).
- Ensure that all customers are treated in a friendly and polite manner so that today's regular customers remain regulars and new customers can be attracted.
- Must take the greatest possible care to ensure accurate accounts, and achieve the highest possible sales by means of intelligent work management and staff training.

Central warehouse supervisors:

- Must guarantee adherence to statutory regulations, safety, smooth operations at lowest costs, best performance and minimum inventory losses in their warehouses.
- Have to keep the warehouse and grounds clean and tidy also.

The personnel and administrative managers:

- Must put the organization and human resources in place in all departments, applying the principle of economy in its extreme form, to enable tasks to be carried out perfectly within the framework of the law and of the company rules.

- Must ensure that the documents and data required by management are available on time.

Relevant to all staff:
- In the course of completing their duties, supervisors must tap into their staff's initiative and ideas.
- The leadership principles to be followed can be deduced from the general management instructions.

Dropping mission statements

Eileen C. Shapiro in her book *Fad Surfing in the Boardroom* closely examines the subject of "mission statements" and describes the successful US steel company Nucor which, as a fantastic success story, was a subject of widespread debate and intensive study. This company had – like ALDI – no written goals. Shapiro found that the mission statements of most companies contained nothing but nonsense. They were full of nice sounding, flowery phrases which most employees did not bother to read and had no connection with the actual processes in the company. Companies with great visions and values do not require mission statements to realize their ambitions.

This also applies perfectly to ALDI. ALDI never had such a statement – and it never needed one. The reason, in my opinion, is as clear and simple as the company's goals themselves: the goals of lowest prices and best quality are simple, understandable, and sensible. What need is there to add anything, in writing or otherwise? Only understandable goals can expect to meet with understanding from the employees.

Despite this, an increasing number of companies are turning to the idea of formulating mission statements. There is no harm in that as long as the process results in a commitment to clear strategies. If these statements convey the meaning and character of the company's activity to all the employees, peg out the scope for action, and channel activities, then written "statements" can also fulfill their purpose. But this is conditional on the goals being written in an "operational" manner so that they can used as guidelines for action, and so that every employee can also make sense of them.

If a company commits itself to a few clear, operational goals that everyone understands and which are clearly worded, there will be no need for anyone to check up on every detail later because they are worried in case things are not working properly. Some of the following examples of mission statements will make this clear.

A major chain store operation in Germany stated its mission as: *"We want to enable people to buy good products at reasonable prices at their convenience."* What can their employees do with sentences like these? Do they contain some operational guideline, a clear directive that solves practical questions?

Another company came up with: *"Recognized value for money and a complete range of products in sophisticated markets with well-trained and motivated employees document our philosophy. We offer our customers everything to cover their daily needs under one roof."* Do all the employees now know exactly what they have to do? Or is this just a matter of nicely worded formalities because nowadays mission statements are the thing to have?

And what would ALDI's statement look like? Perhaps: *"We sell 600 items for people's basic food needs at the best quality and lowest prices anywhere. The prerequisite is rock bottom costs in all areas."* This should tell ALDI employees everything they need to know about daily business. They can act; they can take decisions. This statement is operational, which means it is a basis for action. Clear goals make corporate leadership reliable and easy. Even for projects it would be sensible to think about the real and clear goals at the outset. This makes projects more reliable and faster. Many a project has failed due to a lack of clear goals. Poorly conceived projects smell foul at their inception just as rotten organizations are said to "stink from the head."

More similarity with Toyota than with Tengelmann

Japanese management methods have been under discussion for many years. It is not altogether certain whether everything that comes from Japan originated there, as Robert Townsend explains in *Further up the Organization*. For example, the quality circle had already been invented by IBM prior to 1960. But presumably the Japanese in their obsession with detail simply did an excellent job of copying a lot of things and went on to do them better than the inventors.

German entrepreneurs at the head of mid-sized companies are also familiar with cultures and leadership tools that are very similar to those of ALDI and the Japanese. Owners are less tempted by publicity than hired managers, and that may be one reason why such cultures and leadership methods are much less well known. Herbert H. Bernhardt, owner of the Hamburg-based major paper trading company of the same name, is a prime example. He expresses how he views himself and his cultural standpoint in these words: "I am the foremost servant of my company. My yardstick is: is it in the company's interest?" Many approach their business in the same way, like Klaus Ostendorf, former managing partner of Wendeln, a mass producer of baked goods located in the Emsland city of Garrel in Germany. He and his executives believed "efficiency on details" was the locomotive of their success. He was the head of a company valued in billions of marks, but spent four days per week in the field visiting customers. He spent the fifth day clearing his desk. Quietly this company has grown from a small industrial bakery to the most important in Germany. But it still keeps a low profile.

If you compare Japanese methods with ALDI's, you discover that ALDI is in fact a "Japanese" company, perhaps the "most Japanese" in all Germany. Initially the Japanese companies copied a great deal. You cannot do this without a love of details, and for Japanese companies working on details has always been an essential principle. But then they found their own way, which can be described by the terms *kaizen*, "just in time," *kanban* and "lean management." German chain store operations work differently. Essentially they have little in common with ALDI. So ALDI has more in common with Toyota than with its German competitors Tengelmann and Rewe.

Kaizen at ALDI

Kaizen in particular is a typical ALDI method. Kaizen means the continuous improvement of everything in the company, in particular production and logistics processes. This concept is difficult for many companies to implement, at ALDI a simple solution has been found. Each ALDI company is responsible for specific duties. This means a large number of senior and middle managers are given additional, interesting duties which in other companies are carried out by staff departments.

For example, a warehouse manager at ALDI, in addition to supervising the central warehouse, also takes responsibility for the in-warehouse floor conveyors. He works on achieving continuous improvements, obtains a complete overview of the market, holds discussions with leading manufacturers, and originates organizational improvements of all kinds. For this purpose he may form a small working group with whom he can permanently cooperate. This is how the forklift trucks with initially two and, later, three pallets on the fork – at that time an innovation but now a common sight – first came into use. ALDI could have presumably filed a number of patents.

There must be at least a hundred examples of this procedure at ALDI, such as a sales manager's responsibility for writing the job description for sales managers – and thus for defining the essential duties of a position – or for deciding on the appropriate technical equipment and the size of the refrigerated shelves in the stores.

Trial and error

An outstandingly appropriate method in the kaizen process is "trial and error." It is given special significance because in this way ideas and new methods can be implemented either immediately or at least much more quickly. After some basic deliberation an application is tested immediately in practice before people spend a lot of time precisely analyzing and perfecting it. After the initial test results are obtained, an adaptation or a modification can be made, the test can be called off or postponed.

This method gives people the courage to try something out and perhaps to risk a flop as well. But if something flops, the result – the insight which is gained in the process – is the center of attention rather than the question: "Who is to blame?" There are very few decisions that are right or wrong. Using the "trial and error" method ALDI succeeded in avoiding major catastrophes and mistakes. The widely popular analysis and decision procedures are usually coupled with voluminous analyses that take up the time of many important and highly-paid employees. To fit them in, a meeting with a customer might be dropped, or an employee's appraisal postponed until it is no longer of any use. Many analyses finally land in the shredder – after all, they were highly confidential – or gradually turn yellow in the drawer of one of the top managers.

None of this is new. Eileen C. Shapiro cites in the above-mentioned book a wonderful thought expressed by Mark Twain:

"Continuous improvements are better than delayed perfection."

For all new ideas, developments of a technical or organizational nature, for the introduction of new items, changed qualities or package sizes, ALDI works in compliance with these basic principles.

The "three-store test"

A by-word at ALDI is the "three-store test." These tests are used to try out the potential success of new items or changed package contents and the like. This kind of test tells you fairly accurately nearly everything you need to know, and at the lowest possible effort. This approach has been refined in the past to the extent that that, when the now very popular and attractive non-food promotions were first tested, they were able not only to determine the items' chances of success, but also to estimate the volumes they would need to plan for.

The value of tests should not be underestimated, because the short-comings of a planned measure often do not show up until it has been implemented in practice. The answer is in the doing, not the theorizing – a rapid, radical, but rigorously simple approach.

In a speech on logistics Erwin Conradi, who served for many years as CEO at Metro Cash & Carry, once made a remarkable statement which clearly reflects the low-profile, practical way of thinking at ALDI. This comes as no surprise, since some of the approaches of both companies are identical, and equally important, the excellent earnings that Metro Cash & Carry formerly achieved, made them comparable. The statement was:

"If you feel these principles are too sweeping, trivial, and plain, I would like to point out to you that I have seen many, many more projects fail on so-called 'basics' than on the 'grand design.'"

Personal commitment and passion

The demands which *kaizen* makes on the managers of a company were expressed as follows by its originator, Masaaki Imai. For the highly demanding activity of continuous improvement the "highest degree of personal commitment imaginable is required of the managers." ALDI managers completely exemplify such commitment – not just Theo Albrecht himself, who uses the back of store memos as notepaper.

The passion and determination of the employees are the basis of performance and creativity. The avoidance of waste, demanded at ALDI in the job descriptions as "extremely low costs," is the leading principle. And every manager knows the masses of money and time which in our companies are regularly and truly thrown away: long distances between departments, double work, useless inventory, overly complicated organizational structures, large numbers of long discussions and, finally, disorder and dirt as well.

Daniel Jones, a member of the group of authors which in 1990 published the exciting study on lean production *The Machine That Changed The World*, does not consider high wages to be the main problem in German companies. He commented on a study of organizational structures in Germany with the words:

"The real problems should be sought in poor organization and waste."

By keeping its organization simple and avoiding waste, and exploiting any and all conceivable reserves, ALDI has achieved a superiority which gives it a genuine competitive edge.

Forty years ago Toyota started what today is called lean manufacturing. In answer to the question why it took so long for the Americans to figure out the secrets of the Toyota success, Gary Hamel and C.K. Prahalad have a simple explanation in their book *Competing for the Future*: "The principles practised in Japan contradicted all the assumptions and convictions of the Americans." We could say the same about ALDI, if anyone were to ask why ALDI's competitors still have not decoded ALDI's secrets: *Everything which ALDI did contradicted the assumptions and convictions of German retail managers.* ALDI does everything differently from all the others. And the situation is similar at Toyota. Toyota does nearly everything differently from its competitors and is more successful because of it.

German retail managers, and by now retail managers around the world, when confronted with hard discounters, did not and do not consider it possible to achieve such a high turnover with such a narrow range of products. In addition, outsiders have tremendous difficulty recognizing the cultural elements, and often have even more difficulty understanding them. What the Japanese are doing has little to do with methods and techniques. That is a question of a culture which may suit the Japanese particularly well, but is also practised in western industrial economies – as ALDI shows.

ALDI's reordering system: "Replace whatever is gone"

Many companies maintain complicated inventory control systems and reordering systems based on enormous data management expenditure. At ALDI, on the other hand, this simply works according to the kanban principle, the Japanese approach to inventory control. Simply stated: "replace whatever is gone." The shelf space for one item usually held enough for one week. When the reorder day for this item came up the store manager ordered the amount which had "gone," refilling the shelf. Even though this now is done in some cases at ALDI with computer assistance, the basic approach has not been changed at all. Bookstores operate on a similar simple, but highly intelligent system. Each book contains an inventory card which is removed by the cashier when the book is sold and is used for re-ordering; applying the method "replace whatever is gone."

Decentralization and delegation

The ALDI organizational principles have such a fundamental importance that they leave their mark on the whole corporate culture and form the main basis of the company's success. The core organizational principle consists of delegation and decentralization.

The first and most important decentralization in the ALDI Group was perhaps the decisive one. In the early 1960s the company was divided between Karl Albrecht, with the corporate center of his Southern region in Mülheim an der Ruhr, and his brother Theo Albrecht, whose Northern operation was located in the German city of Essen. This was a decision which probably made possible the company's survival and successful growth. In any case, disputes between the brothers which might have damaged the company were avoided. At Karl Albrecht's ALDI South, family-related conflicts can no longer be expected, neither his son nor his daughter have stayed with the company. At ALDI North under Theo Albrecht, however, both sons have taken on top-level responsibility as members of the administrative board. The design of the family trust may protect the company.

The division of the company allowed the brothers to avoid any disputes involving fundamental strategy. This led, for example, to South maintaining a product range of 450 items, while North expanded to 600 items; later North added refrigerated and frozen foods, while South put the idea on hold; the one had yellow, the other gray floors in their stores, the one was more conservative, the other more experimentally inclined. These decisions were, of course, also influenced by the brothers' immediate employees, the members of the administrative board. But bargaining and unanimous decision making between the brothers were no longer necessary.

Decentralization enables methods, experiences and results to be compared, and creates the freedom to make decisions for or against based on these comparisons. The two ALDI groups have always promoted exchanges of experience, and the separation has substantially increased their wealth of experience. The question here is not so much who is "right" or "wrong," progressive or backward, timid or courageous – there is always more than one right answer. But many companies waste their energy for long periods of time on internal disputes over the right way forward, whilst it is almost impossible to prove whether the one chosen was right or wrong because it is impossible to follow two or more directions at the same time. Another aspect of this question should not be underestimated either: strategic decisions in a company are not exclusively based on hard facts and logic – experience shows that other things play a role: intuition, experience and a "good nose."

Autonomy is less complex

Apparently unconsciously, ALDI also performs one of the essential tasks of organization by its decentralization: reducing the need for communication and coordination as much as possible. The simpler an organization is, the better it can perform. Simplicity requires less management capacity – at least in terms of quantity.

Highly developed structures in business, technology, and society are characterized by a complex network of causal relationships. They are complex, and complex interactions must be organized, and this is usually done with the help of hierarchical structures. Such structures reduce the number of independent units, stand in the way of self-management, and prevent any possible competition between alternative solutions. Administrative rules must be introduced, compliance must be controlled, and "maintaining" these rules, updating and adapting them to changing conditions, ties up substantial capacity: additional departments, staff functions, committees, and experts. Once set in motion, the vicious circle of bureaucratization is rarely broken.

If, therefore, a simple organizational design is successful, it is more intelligent and more effective. The solution lies partly in a sensible under-standing of leadership, but above all in creating small, independent units – in decentralizing. This can also prevent leadership problems caused by unsuitable or second-rate managers. Filling responsible positions in a company with the wrong people can never be prevented; ALDI too has its problems with unsuitable executives. But the effects are much less destructive when units are small and decentralized, and they impact on fewer employees than in one large, centralized organization. The damage which one individual, powerful ruler can do is immense.

Even a company such as ALDI cannot operate exclusively on intelligent systems and guidelines, even at ALDI people play an important role, even here everything repeatedly depends on individuals – how could it be any other way. The point still applies: poor leadership can be compensated for by good organization.

ABB and ALDI: Decentralized and successful

Only a few companies are known to have basic and rigorous decentralization and delegation of duties, responsibility and authority, and at the same time to have arrived at a very simple and easily understood organization. The Swedish-Swiss Group Asea Brown Boveri (ABB), according to experts, has written an eye-opening success story in recent years based on the concept of decentralization. Two hundred thousand employees work in 1,000 individual companies which are divided up, in turn, into profit centers. ABB achieves a return on equity of 20 percent and a return on sales after tax of 10 percent. In retailing the returns on sales are lower due to the greater volume, but in terms of return on equity ALDI easily outperforms the ABB Group.

It is probable that only rigorously decentralized companies and organizations can survive in our complex world. Small instead of large or, as at ABB and ALDI, "small within large." Ant instead of elephant. Small units are more flexible and more adaptable. Several small errors are easier to weather than one "large error" which can be made by one powerful leader. But the chances are also greater that several small units and their managers will produce good ideas and perform well than if they are dependent one personality or one institution. Peter Drucker, in his book *Concept of Corporation* gave consideration to the fundamental significance of decentralization as a principle of organization. Drucker described decentralization not only as a management technique but as the blueprint for a social organization. This becomes clear if you look beyond companies to the constitution of the Federal Republic of Germany or the division of the United States into individual states. These are basic forms of society which I could easily imagine being still more clearly structured and somewhat more decentralized. I believe a company such as ALDI could set an example. What is decisive for the path of centralization or decentralization is how the organizations can be better controlled if they increase in size and complexity. The chart on the next page shows the alternatives.

At ALDI decentralization and delegation go along with clear targets and rules, and are combined with a reasonable amount of control. A very clear example of this is the cell division which is repeatedly carried out at ALDI companies. As soon as a certain number of stores in one region has been reached (roughly 60 to 80 stores) and the distances from the warehouse to the stores needs to be shortened for practical reasons (to a maximum of 50 km) or the warehouse size is already as much as, say, 25,000 square meters of floor space, a split-off in the form of a new company is created. The new entity is complete in itself, including separate bookkeeping, a separate balance sheet and all the functions found in the former company. The increasing competition between ways of handling daily details has frequently led to costs being reduced in absolute terms across all ALDI's decentralized units. Today, in Germany alone the two ALDI groups have 65 regional companies, each of which operates fully independently.

The basic advantages of decentralization can be summarized as follows: small units are characterized by

- less complexity and
- less need to communicate, plus
- better local market knowledge;
- new people can develop independently:
- small, easily manageable units breed fewer conflicts;
- the sales assistant knows the general manager;
- a feeling of community develops better in small units;
- details become more important, and
- a larger variety of ideas are developed;
- in every way, there is more concentration on less work,
- unexpected problems can be handled more quickly;
- problem areas can be better isolated;
- the group's individual businesses are involved in healthy competition with each other;
- even the cooperation with the Works Council may be better.

Centralization or decentralization?

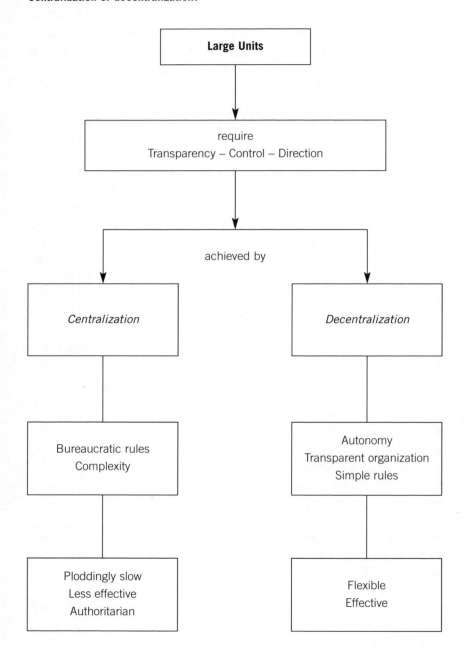

Union officials and public opinion makers frequently maintain that ALDI's policies of rigorous decentralization and "cell division" are motivated by the desire to avoid compulsory disclosure laws and circumvent the requirement in Germany to establish Group-wide works councils. But these are merely welcome side benefits, not the motives.

So the assessment contained in the following article in *manager magazin* 4/84, does not get to the heart of the matter:

"New ALDI companies were always formed when existing regional centers were threatened by compulsory disclosure due to growth. For example Berlin: . . .Theo Albrecht divided ALDI GmbH & Co. KG into two companies – one ALDI GmbH & Co. Berlin Nord KG and one ALDI GmbH & Co. Berlin Süd KG. The move did not make economic or logistical sense, but it did help to block any indiscreet interest in turnover and revenues."

In fact, that change was due to an urgent need to expand the central warehouse on the north side of Berlin. But that was not possible because there was no additional land available. So the cell division referred to was carried out because there was no option available at the original location. Of course, substantial logistical advantages arose from this, especially in a heavily congested big city, because the new structure meant that drivers coming from the north or south never needed to go further than the city center. But outsiders are not in a position to assess the organizational advantages of a cell division. Between the two Berlin companies, a kind of sporting competition broke out reminiscent of New York baseball as to who would achieve the best results and performance, a competition which had neither to be ordered or subtly initiated but which simply developed from employees' desire to perform well. And that happened despite the fact that some patience was always shown toward performance in Berlin because it was known that all the conditions in such a large city were much more unfavorable than in other regions of western Germany. But as was discovered, this was largely based on a poor estimate of the available reserves.

Today, a general tendency toward more decentralization and delegation can be observed; the ideal case appears to be the factually separated and independently operated companies as separate legal entities with full responsibility for their business operations – but within the framework of a shared group strategy. Large companies are going mid-size again; central management is being dismantled.

In principle, ALDI has always been a mid-sized company and has remained so. Size itself is not decisive, but the appropriate size. What counts is not sales figures, but market share.

Delegation and control

Corporate executives and top managers repeatedly argue against extensive delegation and decentralization by saying that centralization at one location simplifies control, and is even a precondition for that control. Critics believe that rigorous decentralization leads to double work and therefore double costs. Having the same function performed in two physically separated regional units is a situation which many completely reject. Besides, they feel that you can keep a better eye on employees in one location. Many companies could never imagine implementing the kind of decentralization practised so widely by ALDI, which extends even to bookkeeping and accounting. But here the critics of rigorous decentralization are falling prey to a fallacy: if at one location, within a given period of time, ten million pieces of data are generated, they will be more difficult to control than one million pieces of data received at each of ten locations.

Experience generally shows that mistakes and problem areas involved are more easily isolated in a decentralized system, if only due to the fact that – taking ALDI's operating companies as an example – there are 30 independent results which do not need to be analyzed as one enormous, opaque pot.

A lot of time and nerve are required before companies can bring themselves to move on to new organizational pastures. The *FAZ* (Frankfurter Allgemeine Zeitung, one of Germany's largest, serious daily newspapers) reported about the REWE Group on 2 March 1995:

"The pressure on the margins impacted more on the Rewe chain store outlets than the independent Rewe retailers: while the captive stores showed losses of 10 to 15 percent, the independent retailers were able either to maintain or even increase their operating profits. Since these independent operators can evidently react more quickly and more flexibly to the market, Rewe is now delegating greater entrepreneurial authority to the employed branch managers . . ."

Finally, people are beginning to understand which way the wind is blowing. What remains, however, is the difficult task of implementation. One well-known retail manager once told me: "Store managers cannot do that." What he meant was that they could not be granted the limited freedom of selecting items from the central list of a chain operation. This statement is based on a certain perception of people which in fact does not permit delegation and does not recognize the connections between motivation, performance and success. In practice, there is no shortage of antiquated ideas about the motivation of employees and managers, such as that employees have to be "motivated" by means of praise and a complicated system of incentives. These and similar ideas were already examined and discarded decades ago by Frederick Herzberg. And Reinhard Sprenger, in his bestselling *The Myth of Motivation*, has very effectively brought the fatal consequences of convictions of this kind to the attention of many German managers.

Delegation means sharing power

Managers at ALDI have shared out some of their authority, their power, to their employees. Power concentrated in the hands of a few is thus avoided and many more employees can participate in a real way, i.e. responsibly, in the company's development. In a company which is success-oriented, superiors can simply not afford to do without the participation of their employees. Whether the superiors also use their opportunities and meet their obligations to cooperate can be very easily determined at ALDI as part of the supervision process.

The vehicle for transferring this power is the job description. Basically, a certain amount of skepticism towards too many written rules and over-detailed job descriptions is healthy. It can be simplified even further than the ALDI way. In principle, however, it is right to clearly regulate the core duties and decision-making powers by describing these duties or jobs. This provides a secure environment for the true application of delegation. Regulations such as these should not contain a great deal of detail. Instead, they should be goal-oriented and fairly broadly worded.

Decentralization by means of continually setting up new companies which have their own headquarters (warehouse, vehicle fleet, administration) leads to power sharing at ALDI. You do not find small, weak companies and large, powerful ones; all are given equal "support." This system has contributed to relatively conflict-free work in the organization. There are no dominant centers of power, and it is unusual for employees to delegate upwards. The system functions nearly without any friction. At ALDI you won't find the squabbles over authority which can be frequently observed in other businesses, the familiar power struggles. Things are clear, reasonable, and they are checked by the supervisors. There are also checks on whether the individual supervisors permit their people to take decisions and act in conformance with their job descriptions.

Companies which, like supermarket chains, are in principle already decentralized, can maintain and boost their competitiveness by giving more authority to their local employees who are in direct contact with customers. But often they simply do not have the courage. Due to the very wide variety and broad scope of duties performed by employees in contact with customers in other companies there is even more creative freedom than at ALDI, with its fairly fixed sales conditions. Organizational design at these companies is much more decisive for their competitiveness than it is at ALDI.

The "Harzburg Model"

In terms of form and organization, delegation at ALDI works along the lines of the "Harzburg Model." This system of delegating duties, authority and responsibility has shaped ALDI so much that it merits being discussed here in detail. Some things may give the impression of exaggerated order and bureaucracy, but the system fitted ALDI very well, and its well thought-out application also led to a lean organization.

The Führungsakademie der Wirtschaft (Business Leadership Academy) in Bad Harzburg, headed by its founder Professor Reinhard Höhn, was for many years a leading institution in Germany for executive education and training. The Academy, which has produced some famous college professors, developed a complete leadership model called the "Harzburg Model."

At the center of the model is the principle of rigorous delegation. That means that three things must be delegated concurrently:

- the task,
- the authority necessary to perform this task, and
- the responsibility for its execution and results.

What is delegated and why? Tasks are delegated which
- others can perform better,
- others can perform more cost-effectively,
- make the job more interesting for the employee,
- include responsibility,

- can be viewed by employees as a challenge and an opportunity to add to their qualifications,
- relieve supervisors to focus on their core tasks and permit them to avoid unnecessary time pressure.

Moreover, the following principles apply:
- The task is delegated to an employee on the ground (close to customer) who is also entrusted with its execution.
- The management limits itself to setting rough guidelines and agreements on objectives to avoid individual instructions and individual orders.
- Performance is checked by spot checks and evaluation of results.
- Upward delegation is not accepted

Responsibility for management and actions

However, it is easy to make mistakes in the implementation of the delegation model. It can only function if all the elements are in place. A distinction is drawn between *management responsibility*, which relates to supervisory responsibilities toward employees, and *responsibility for action*, which pertains to fulfilling certain duties. *Task and authority* taken together are specified in a job description as a general *set of objectives* for the position. The following example gives excerpts from a job description of an ALDI sales manager to whom five to six district managers report who, in turn, have six to eight store managers reporting to them.

Job description for a sales manager

I. Job designation
Sales Manager

II. Subordination
He reports to the general manager.

III. Supervision
He supervises the district managers.
He is the disciplinary supervisor of the store managers.

IV. Objectives of position
The position-holder must ensure through his actions that the highest possible

turnover is achieved in his sales area on a permanent basis. He must ensure smooth business operations in tidy sales outlets at the lowest costs as well as the highest possible performance levels and accurate books, to maintain and improve existing competitiveness.

As part of his work the position-holder is expected to appoint store managers capable of meeting the requirements of the position and to ensure that the district managers reporting to them carry out their duties in compliance with the job descriptions.

In the fulfillment of his duties he must utilize the initiative and contributions of his employees. The applicable management principles are based on the General Management Guidelines.

V. Duties

The position-holder must personally discharge the following professional duties:

1 He takes decisions on the hiring and firing of store managers and potential store managers as well as on the contents of references.

   He must observe the labor laws. In case of doubt he can obtain advice from the personnel and administrative managers.

2 He approves salaries and benefits of the store managers.

3 He decides on the induction of district managers.

4 He writes a performance review of each district manager every year and discusses it with the individuals concerned.

5 He approves the breakdown into district manager areas.

6 He approves vacations, deputies and the suspension of district managers.

7 He determines the layouts of the stores and approves the arrangement of merchandise groups.

8 He decides in which stores renovation work should be carried out.

9 He approves repairs and the purchase of fixtures and fittings up to a price of euro 2,500.00.

10 He advises the general manager on district manager salaries.

11 He provides advice for the building and planning of stores.

12 He makes suggestions on which items to list or delist.

13 He advises the general manager on the scope and plan of flyer advertising and special promotions at the individual stores.

14 He advises the general manager on opening hours.

Of course there are general rules for some decisions, such as setting salaries. The duty of supervisors in the context of delegation is to check up that their staff are capably performing the functions stated in their job descriptions as well as fulfilling their leadership duties as supervisors.

In many companies many managers have particular difficulties with leadership duties. These basically involve very simple interactions. Leadership involves:

- negotiating objectives with the employee,
- training him and developing him in such a way that he is capable of fulfilling his duties, and
- checking on employees to establish whether and how well they are fulfilling their duties and their responsibilities.

The work of the senior management is assessed in writing as part of an annual performance review by the relevant supervisor. The levels of performance are ranked from 1 to 10. The assessment factors are:

- professional knowledge relevant to the job
- willingness to work
- performance of duties relating to delegation and individual tasks
- conscientiousness
- forward thinking and acting
- ability to explain things
- intensive handling of their range of duties (improvements, suggestions, above-average successes)
- activities as supervisor
- performance of delegation overall.

"Supervision" and performance control

Checking contributes to meeting targets, makes the business more secure and – perhaps most importantly – opens important contacts between supervisors and their people. The *checks* take the form of work supervision and performance control. Supervision involves spot checks of a defined scope that are performed at set intervals. In concrete terms, at ALDI this is arranged so that all supervisors basically do spot checks on how each of their employees is performing in relation to three tasks or subject areas every month. These review points should be carefully selected and therefore ought to be already planned at the beginning of the month. This should also prevent supervisors from going looking for mistakes, by failing to specify what they want to check until they are carrying out the review, and then only describing the errors they find as review points. Or they may simply start looking for mistakes inspired by the thought: if you look hard enough, you'll find something. Annual performance controls, on the other hand, check on the growth of significant ratios in comparison to the previous year or in comparison to other departments or other ALDI companies.

Thanks to the monthly supervision, surprises during the annual performance controls become highly unlikely. That is why Höhn emphasized the significance of supervision compared with performance control when he stated: "Performance control is long term, it can sometimes turn out to be an autopsy." I am convinced that if all companies applied the principle of supervisory checks properly, the likelihood of such catastrophes as the bankruptcy at Barings Bank in London, which was plunged into a life-threatening crisis by the irresponsible speculation of one of its senior managers in Singapore, would be greatly reduced.

What must be rejected is a checking process, and most importantly a certain type of checking *behavior* which is not based fundamentally on trust – trust in the ability of employees to handle their tasks. Without such fundamental trust, successful work is difficult to imagine. Trust is also an absolute prerequisite for reducing complexity. The sociologist Niklas Luhmann encapsulated this thought in the subtitle of his book *Trust: a mechanism for reducing social complexity*. The absence of trust renders checking measures absurd. Taking complete responsibility, after careful consideration and based on firm conviction, employees must be selected for defined positions and empowered with the authority they require. There should be no doubt as to whether they can carry out their tasks. Employees generally only perform at their best when they sense, and know, that they enjoy the confidence of their supervisors.

But checks in this sense – as a feedback procedure and as a dialog between supervisor and employees – also means determining how *well* the employee is working – not only what mistakes he or she has made. This form of check is intended to help the employee, the supervisor and the company to enhance performance. It promotes cooperation and shows employees what their supervisors and their company consider important. Last but not least, checks thus also mean showing an interest in employee performance. The Fraunhofer Institute has determined that 75% of employees complain that they get no feedback from their supervisors, who do not acknowledge their achievements.

German companies should take note of the report of 6 June 1997 in the *Lebensmittel-Zeitung* about the behavior of Erwin Conradi, then chairman of Metro's supervisory board:

Conradi fires DIY store manager

During a tour of three "Praktiker" do-it-yourself supply outlets in Mönchengladbach last week, the chairman of the Metro Board of Directors, Erwin Conradi, found unacceptable conditions in one of the stores. As part of his store-check program Conradi will be visiting all the Metro Group's distribution channels.

Such "store checks" are the ALDI way. Like Conradi, ALDI top management also carries out detailed review programs in the stores, establishes the facts on the ground and writes assessments. ALDI managers as well, apparently, as Metro managers are capable of doing this because they know the details. Only "firing" is handled differently at ALDI, but it is probably not done at Metro Cash & Carry as depicted above either.

A simple example from my own experience may help to illustrate how these kinds of situations can be handled. As general manager at ALDI in Schleswig-Holstein I was the supervisor of the sales manager. The tasks of the sales manager included making decisions about repairs in the stores. But a number of other tasks involved expenses and costs. So the work supervision point I selected was to review "the costs approved by the sales manager in the month of September." On the planned date I asked the sales manager to come to my office – very often such meetings took place in his office as well – and requested the file containing the cost receipts for the month of September from bookkeeping.

Together we leafed through the file. Whenever a receipt bearing his signature turned up we paused. Mostly these were some sort of routine expenses which were of little interest to us. But there were also repeatedly bills for repairing the machines used to clean the floors in our stores. Costs for the wages of the manufacturer's mechanic, wages for traveling time to and from the store, mileage allowance, as well as charges for spare parts. After we had seen a whole series of such bills we went back through the receipts a second time and tallied up the total costs. We discovered that the repair costs for these machines were unexpectedly high. What could be done – in view of the fact that the machines were in good running order and these sort of repairs could hardly be avoided? That was the decisive question for this supervisory review.

After discussing the matter together we came to the conclusion that the repairs should be handled by our own mechanics at the central warehouse, especially to lower the high traveling costs of the manufacturer's mechanics. We bought two spare machines which we kept in the central warehouse and which we could then have brought to any store by our own supply trucks with the next regular delivery if a machine broke down. This allowed us to achieve substantial savings. The solution was so good and so simple that it was taken on board later by all other ALDI companies.

I have deliberately picked out a positive example of *how* such checks, which are frequently seen as unpleasant, can be carried out. Admittedly there were also other examples and other situations. But what I am concerned with here is the principle which – rightly understood and sensibly implemented – takes the positive and negative aspects of employee performance into account in equal measure. In general, ALDI managers were experts in checking techniques due to their intensive and long-standing practice with this system.

Checking on the general managers

The ALDI checking system is not restricted to store managers and employees, the general managers' work is also reviewed from time to time. The higher body, the administrative board, is responsible for this. This system will be described in detail below, because I feel that the way ALDI executives are assessed can be transferred to other companies as well.

First, the tasks which a general manager must carry out himself, his *functions*, should be distinguished. These can be checked directly. But it is primarily those tasks which he is called upon to perform as a supervisor, his *leadership tasks*, which must be reviewed.

The *functions* of the general manager listed in the job description include:

- the hiring of senior managers,
- deciding on pay levels and schedules for wages and salaries,
- deciding on the use of advertising budget and on any construction work at stores costing more than euro 5,000 and
- the leasing of new stores (location, lease payments, terms of contract),
- deciding on the purchase and sale of trucks, and
- chairing the district manager meetings.

Review points related to these functions could, for example, include the following, with the performance of the tasks being subject as a rule to generally binding rules and provisions such as: "New stores should have at least 600m^2 of sales space."

- Which district managers were hired over the last six months? By examining the personnel files and the documents they contain it is possible to assess the conditions under which people are hired.
- How was the last raise in salary for senior managers justified? On the basis of personal assessment or achievements? In this context, the achievements of certain employees can be reviewed by examining performance results and making comparisons.
- What advertising media were put to use in the past two months? How much advertising was done? How much did specific advertising media cost? How many suppliers were contacted? How extensively and for what reasons was advertising by flyer carried out for certain stores?
- What reconstruction decisions were made in the previous quarter? Why and how was the construction work carried out? The relevant cost calculations can be checked. Were quotations obtained from different builders?
- Were the general guidelines observed when store locations were leased? This includes the inspection of the new location and forming a personal opinion about the quality of the location.
- When trucks were sold in the previous year how much mileage did they have on them? Are there trucks that regularly incur high repair costs, which it would be better to offload now? What sizes of trucks were bought and what did they cost? Were there any special negotiating conditions and successes?
- How the general manager chairs the district manager meetings can be assessed by participating in a meeting and assessing it on the basis of its agenda, atmosphere, results, communication processes, and whether all the district managers are actively involved.

The *leadership tasks* can be inferred from the general requirements. They include:

- permitting employees to work and make decisions independently within the scope of their job descriptions,
- management by objectives
- delegation of special duties,
- reviewing the performance results (performance control)
- carrying out regular employee supervision.

Moreover, a general manager's leadership ability and behavior can also be measured indirectly by the company's profits and the successes of individual employees. How fast and how well individual business decisions are implemented can reflect the manager's performance.

A very good indicator of the behavior and ability of managers is the work supervision the supervisor carries out with his employees. From the results of the review, which must be recorded in writing, a number of points can be established including:

- How were the supervision points selected?
- Which findings did the supervisor make solely on the basis of the facts?
- How did he assess the results?
- How are criticism and recognition worded?
- How did he word the findings?
- Were any interesting, new aspects revealed during the review?

The reviewing supervisor – in the case of the general manager this is the administrative board – can, however, also look at individual areas of the business. Here are a few examples, from throughout the company, which can give a good sense of the company's situation and permit an assessment of how well the general manager is meeting the objectives defined in his job description. Such a review can involve:

- Questions regarding the manager's most recent supervision review by the administrative board.
- A general exchange of ideas with the general manager about corporate leadership, questions involving authority, his employees and about interaction with his team in general. What is not working well?
- A review of the implementation of decisions made by the company's management.
- The examination of minutes of meetings.
- A joint analysis of the most recent business comparison, of the employee reviews, of the results of bonus systems, their usefulness and successes.
- The analysis of labor court proceedings and investment decisions as well as the staff turnover in certain employee groups.
- Questions regarding the general manager's knowledge of certain company issues or certain performance figures which he really should be familiar with.
- The handling of customer complaints and
- The assessment of newly leased stores.
- Visits by the general manager, the sales manager and the district manager to the stores and an analysis of their findings.
- Examination and assessment of the supervision reviews of various employees to determine how the leadership techniques are used in the company in general

and what sort of leadership style is practised. Conclusions about the atmosphere in the company can also be drawn from this.

- An analysis of certain cost categories within a defined period.
- An analysis of truck log books.
- The organization of warehouse departments.
- An inspection and assessment of various aspects of the stores (cash management, cleanliness of all rooms including back rooms, merchandise planning behavior, stock freshness checks, and many more).

Initially the results should be simply recorded in a descriptive manner. A follow-up assessment can result if the checkpoint calls for it. From the discussions during the joint reviews with the general manager, useful insights contributed by either party can arise for the management of the whole group. Such a review should take place on the basis of a friendly relationship, not secretly. The reviewers must be well aware that perfection is impossible and that new insights are frequently only possible due to mistakes.

It is apparent that the reviews can be very detailed. But these comprehensive spot checks which the administrative board of the ALDI Group regularly carries out at the actual stores and facilities provide an accurate picture of the company and its management team. Attention is focused here on the avoidance of any kind of waste in the sense of what the Japanese refer to as muda. The key questions have to be: Where can something be improved? Where can misdirected developments be avoided? Spot checks are much more effective and cheaper than permanent checking systems and routine checks.

At this point we should remind ourselves once again that some major or minor business disasters could have been prevented if the companies concerned had operated in this way. The risks taken by Deutsche Bank with its loans to property speculator Jürgen Schneider, whose business dealings culminated in 1 billion euros' worth of debt, could have been limited by an intelligent spot check system. Jürgen Krumnow, a member of bank's board of directors, said at the trial before the Frankfurt District Court that he had to assume that, naturally, all the details had been examined. Anything else would have implied distrust of the employees who had presented these documents to him. I consider this position to be basically wrong. The senior managers at Deutsche Bank are entitled to have their directors take an interest in how they perform their tasks and to have their work formally reviewed of their work y the board from time to time. This might have resulted in interesting and revealing discussions about the loan relationship. Work on details; do not fear checks. A check does not imply mistrust, hunting for mistakes or meting out punishments. At ALDI, work supervision and delegation were essential factors in the company's success. No major catastrophes occurred.

Very frequently supervisors experience the obligation of checking up as more unpleasant than their employees do, as a burdensome obligation.[22] Many feel out of their depth when carrying them out, too. There are deep-seated reasons for this resistance: executives are afraid of unpleasant discussions to clear up the facts and do not know how to phrase any criticism they may need to convey to their employees. Supervisors are especially insecure when they are supposed to judge the leadership behavior of their employees, one of the most important tasks of a supervisor. The avoidance of checks and criticism becomes the avoidance of responsibility.

A few months after a presentation about his review system the production manager of a well-known machine construction company called me. He had been applying my suggestion at work for some time. And his best result was: "I have re-established a close and genuine relationship to my employees and I am genuinely back into my work." For me this was a thoughtful word of thanks.

To handle their tasks and meet their responsibilities, supervisors must learn checking techniques. Important suggestions also emerge here for the responsibility and tasks of supervisory boards of stock companies.

The Harzburg Model, as used by ALDI, was heavily criticized in later years and quickly fell out of favor in modern management culture. The actual criticism, however, was directed against an excess of bureaucracy which, in my opinion, was also completely superfluous. It was created by the "business enthusiasm" which quickly develops at such academies. They always want more, something new, a new offer, another important issue. ALDI did not work that bureaucratically.

Practical line work instead of theoretical staff work

Its clear line orientation is a very decisive difference between ALDI and those companies who work with staff departments focused on specific functions. At ALDI there are no staff departments – and for a good reason: staff work is superfluous. It is much more effective to assign all tasks to line managers, to those directly involved in practical business processes, especially the direct responsibility for the practicable implementation and application. This gives these employees an opportunity to directly test their ideas without having to ask someone in advance. This prevents loss of time and long-drawn-out implementation processes. In addition, such a structure leads to fewer problems with the acceptance of innovations than when these changes come from the desks of theoreticians at headquarters.

New suggestions at ALDI used to be discussed at meetings of the individual groups, such as the warehouse managers, and proposed for use. All general managers received minutes of such discussions so that they were able to get an idea of all the points discussed for themselves, even if for no other reason than to be able to check the implementation in their own businesses at a later date. Issues of overriding importance for which a warehouse manager did not have sufficient authority were presented to the general manager meeting for decision making. Now such meetings of warehouse managers and sales managers have been discontinued, but the principle still operates in a similar way.

Helmut Maucher, former Nestlé CEO, confirmed in a presentation[23] on this subject something that has always been ALDI's practice:

"People who do not know what they want need an army of staff workers to write down what he should want. You could ask some departments: 'Are you helping us with the solution, or are you part of the problem?' We have too many experts who are precisely analyzing why everything is so rotten without making a single suggestion about improvements or how they might be implemented."

One staff position, which in some retail companies is considered indispensable, is the audit department, which performs checks in the stores to take some of the strain off line managers – district managers and sales managers. But they are not only relieved of this work but of their responsibility as well, and that is the decisive design flaw. The supervisors themselves have to audit their stores and employees as part of their supervisory duties, and work with them on a basis of trust. They do not need any agents who interfere in their working relationships and, what's more, who have imperfect knowledge and insufficient information. The usefulness of audit departments is also questionable. This staff work would be better in the hands of the individual line managers. The book-keeping or a statistical department can supply the basic data.

What remains decisive is that the practical and responsible workers come up with solutions. Their direct responsibility for day-on-day performance alone is a guarantee of responsible thinking and suggestions. After all, they are the ones who will be affected by the consequences in their daily work.

A lot of waste could be avoided in companies if the employees were, for example, included in quality circles. One example: an important shipbuilding company has accepted an important major contract. It is under tremendous time pressure and all indicators seem to point to the impossibility of meeting the deadline. Those working on the job know the reasons for the delays and how the pace of work can be accelerated. But they are not asked. So everyone goes on muddling through. In the end, the company requires one and a half years to complete the project. A Canadian competitor completes the exact same project in only five months. The only reason for the difference: a more intelligent organization. The German company's employees were quite familiar with the details of this organization. But nobody asked them. Responsibility and authority were not in their hands but in the hands of the planning department and the top management. The example illustrates the untapped resources of individual companies.

Line managers, unlike self-perpetuating staff departments, do not have the time for extensive, written elaborations. Clarity and understanding are supported by short reports. Short reports compel the writer to have an eye for the essentials. The frequently recommended "one-page memos" do not contain many figures to discuss. When figures are kept to a minimum it is easier to check their reliability. They inspire greater confidence. The American writer John Steinbeck once said that the first step toward writing a novel is to write a one-page statement of purpose.

Creativity and the ignorance requirement

At ALDI the number of statistics is so few they can nearly be counted on one hand. They are simple, manageable and comprehensible, and not a bit scientific. Only the most vital data are prepared for the internal auditing and information system. You can still see the forest despite the daunting number of trees.

ALDI does not require any data gathering and analyses to establish the "direct product profitability" of each item. At ALDI they know what information is important to the business, and they can focus on it. While their competitors are fervently analyzing stacks of numbers or keeping their most important employees busy creating budgets, ALDI has long finished its thinking and has implemented the results.

It boggles the mind how difficult many executives find it to pursue their objectives based on a few, essential figures. Thanks to today's modern analysis tools and highly sophisticated data processing methods you can obtain any data imaginable and combine them in any imaginable way. And then you can cling on to them wonderfully well in a nice warm office. Many managers, in Turkey for example, love to think through the theory on the basis of enormous quantities of numbers. The warehouse manager of an ALDI-like organization loves his personal computer which he does not need in his work. In many corporate centers, retail managers still visualize their customers in terms of market shares, average purchases and customer receipt analyses from the scanner cash registers which provide a breakdown of sales at different times of day and at different locations. They work at shelf optimization programs and customer walking distance studies. But *why* the customer buys *this* item remains unknown.

The main contradictions in the philosophy of corporate leadership are also clearly revealed when you compare the American success stories Wal-Mart and General Electric. ALDI does everything differently from its competitors. ALDI is also different from Wal-Mart with its 100-terabyte data warehouse. Wal-Mart analyzes everything, ALDI only some things. This fact is also a confirmation of the notion that ALDI bears a greater similarity with the Toyotas and GEs of this world than with its own direct competitors. ALDI follows exactly the course outlined by Jack Welch: "Everyone wants to put all the data that they can think of on a page. My idea is, simplify it. Enrich the language; that carries the day, not the paper. There's no tradeoff in terms of the information content, not for me, because I can't do anything with all the information. It doesn't help most people at the next level to have all that data. What they need to know is, what are the strategic questions I have to answer? What are the variables?"

It might be useful for those in the planning and control departments, which are large in every company, and in the executive offices where statistics are interpreted, to consider a very basic insight formulated by Gerd Binnig, German Nobel laureate in physics (for his work on the scanning tunnel microscope):

"Creative work requires a certain degree of ignorance."

The "ignorance" meant here is doing without information. People who fill themselves with knowledge have a thorough understanding of what already exists, but have little capacity left for creating anything new.

There are plenty of data, but there is a shortage of information and orientation. How do you retrieve information for decision making from thousands of records? For example, improved information on cost structures is constantly being demanded. Many ingenious attempts are made, costs are distributed according to apparently intelligent methods to cost units and cost centers. In retailing the "direct product profitability method" enjoyed a boom for some years – but it was a system which led many managers in trade and industry astray. Infinite amounts of data were and still are collected, processed and used as a basis for decision making. As experience has shown, without any success. In the meantime, the "direct product profitability method" has evidently been given a quiet burial. What was this concept all about?

Excursus: Direction product profitability (DPP)

Invented in the United States, intensively cultivated in Germany by Rewe-Leibbrand, supported by active producers, for some time DPP held a fascination for business managers similar to today's "efficient consumer response" (ECR). Knowing product profitability was supposed to supply the suitable criterion for decisions on product range policy. Essentially, this approach means retaining the items returning high profits and eliminating low earners. DPP was also meant to bring transparency to the product range and to a company's cost and profit structures. DPP is a cost unit accounting system for establishing the revenues and costs of an item and allocating them directly to it. Warehouse and vehicle fleet costs, i.e. logistics costs, the store lease, the interior store furnishings, personnel costs, interest on inventory and the energy costs are included in the allocation.

Such attempts are nothing new in business economics. Companies often need a basis for their pricing. But there are few sectors where price is more firmly determined by the market than in food retailing. In addition the procurement costs, i.e. the purchase prices, directly provide you with the allocation of 70 to 80 percent of an item's costs. Whether it really makes sense in this context to allocate the store lease at 2 percent or vehicle-related costs of 0.8 percent to an individual item is highly questionable. Apart from this, even in a purely theoretical sense, an accurate allocation of costs to their sources is impossible, or even unacceptable. The lease of a store is paid as a fixed cost, independent of the product range or even the rate of turnover of an item.

But apart from the theoretical and practical difficulties, the most important question remaining is whether such allocation acrobatics actually make sense. Crowds of consultants and the Food Marketing Institute (FMI) in the United States are vying with one another to prove to retailers what a pioneering development is taking place in this area, one which is both revolutionary and necessary for survival in the marketplace.

Computers were fed with extensive material, but they did not answer the question of how product ranges are really defined. The company's retail concept is of primary importance here, and is also answerable for what attracts customers to a specific store in the first place.

Once that is settled, the assortment policy is pretty much determined. The purchaser then negotiates with suppliers and decides in favor of a certain item at a certain price. It is totally unimaginable that the lease or energy costs incurred by a can of "best quality peas" or even the labor costs and the 20 centimeters of shelf space it requires could have any say in the matter at all. Even for the company's pricing strategy, it is pretty much irrelevant whether the can of peas causes 8 percent of store costs and the box of diapers 17 percent (as a percentage of their respective sales). Market prices just cannot be ignored. A number of companies have calculated themselves out of the market with faulty reckonings and inappropriate cost accounting. This is evidently also the reason why the direct product profitability method was buried again after a few years.

Focusing on the essentials

Initially, DPP got everyone excited – with the exception of one organization: ALDI. ALDI did not even notice what was going on because the company was focusing on issues which were genuinely appropriate for increasing sales or reducing costs. ALDI adhered to the ideas of Gerd Binnig, though it was probably unaware of the fact: not too many numbers and analyses, rather, think about concrete interrelationships and about how one can achieve higher sales to customers.

In many companies, however, the days of bloated analyses are gradually drawing to a close. They are becoming leaner, and middle management is losing some of its tasks and some of its jobs. Having less time for your own work can be a good thing if it really compels people to confine their efforts to the essentials and to prioritize, because they have no other choice. It would make sense to carve out a block of time to talk to employees and colleagues. In some companies a disturbing new practice has arisen. Discussions are being replaced by e-mail communication between supervisors and their employees. Finding time to talk, however, also means focusing on the essentials and cutting out all those endless meetings. Daniel Goeudevert even suggests replacing the many seated sessions into standing sessions.

The lean information system at ALDI is also reflected in the fact that employees are only informed about what is immediately related to their own work. This may contradict some modern approaches to employee involvement but it is an integral part of ALDI culture. It has enabled ALDI to ensure that competitors and the public have very little hard information about the ALDI Group and, aside from the members of the administrative boards in Essen and Mülheim, hardly anyone knows the sales figures achieved by the two groups today, either in Germany or abroad. That may not matter now, but it was a decisive competitive factor in the early years. Many competitors merely shook their heads over this nonsensical sales concept. If they had known the figures this nonsense was producing, some would undoubtedly reacted differently, not just sticking their heads in the sand or arrogantly ignoring the newcomer and continuing as before.

Statistics and internal competition: ALDI's internal benchmarking

An essential leadership tool was repeatedly making clear to all employees in discussions, meetings or through job descriptions that top achievements and continuous improvements were expected. These achievements were also measured, for example as productivity ratios such as sales per employee in stores, warehouses, the vehicle fleet as well as operational and time comparisons of all performance and cost parameters between the individual departments or sales districts or between the individual ALDI companies. The time comparison with preceding months and preceding years is also an essential control tool with which the relative developments can be tracked and evaluated in addition to the comparison between operating areas.

This creates a competition that sets benchmarks and makes any management accounting/control department or other standard target-setting procedures such as budgets and planning forecasts superfluous. Comparing actual figures means comparing facts with facts instead of desired figures and guesstimates on the one hand with real figures on the other. Revenues and costs, expressed in money, are useful yardsticks.

And it makes more sense to carefully study, and question, a few figures than to produce every conceivable relationship between masses of figures by computer. Computer-generated number dumps are not suitable for corporate management.

People like achievement because it gives their activity a purpose, especially if it is related to successes. If a company can communicate this purpose that defines and recognizes achievements, this creates an additional cultural element. In the end these achievements have an impact as greater competitiveness for the ALDI Group and broader market and customer acceptance. This makes sense, and it can also boost employees' pride in their individual achievements. I believe this is also an explanation of why ALDI cashiers, despite their strenuous work, are considered the friendliest in the retail business. As representatives of their company they experience the customers' appreciation of the company's efforts on a daily basis. It was even said that ALDI in early years had a significant positive impact on the inflation rate in the former West Germany. This is something that employees can feel proud of, since it was their achievement.

ALDI's approach can be applied to other companies:
- develop simple and clear overviews of basic data,
- no applied overhead,
- no distribution key.
- Instead, establish yardsticks such as time comparisons or comparisons of operations or units within operations.

Do not allocate the insurance bills that are paid in January for the whole year to all twelve months but show them in the profit & loss account for January. Then anyone reading the balance sheets will get a clear picture of what is going on. His attention is caught and he can ask the appropriate questions. The facts are not leveled out and their significance is not obscured to the point of invisibility. Such a statement in statistics and balance sheets induces readers to examine the bills themselves.

Data processing should also be approached strategically. Directions of thrust must be determined, the potential for insights must be defined. In short: less is more.

It is questionable whether the "total" analysis of customer receipts comprising thousands of data can really be a source of practically applicable information. Ultimately, human beings have to realize the significance of the links forged by information technology and make decisions. The number of options for analysis approaches infinity. But the conclusions from them must be quickly grasped and applied by the people who are obliged to offer services to the customer in their daily work.

Before seizing the next kilometer of computer print-outs (which will explain everything . . .) or setting out to march through the myriad paths of the data warehouse, it might be better in the supermarket to consider for a moment whether the price difference between the 500g pack and the 250g pack of Jacobs-Krönung (the most famous German coffee brand, manufactured by Kraft-Foods makes sense against the background of an overall consideration of business targets, the issue of single person households, or absolute gross earnings.

In many stores we can find the following price differentials:
Jacobs Krönung 500g pack euro 4.00
100 grams = euro 0.80
Jacobs Krönung 250g pack euro 3.25
100 grams = euro 1.30

***After subtracting the purchase price the stores are left
with the following absolute margins for 100 grams:***
Jacobs Krönung 500g pack 10 cents
Jacobs Krönung 250g pack 23 cents

It this requires some thinking, work on details and, most importantly, creativity, to determine the preferred price strategy. In view of the trend toward single-person households, which makes it seem necessary to carry the small pack, and in addition the end consumer price of the large pack is determined by tough competition, it might make sense to lower the price of the small package by as much as euro 0.32 to a theoretical minimum of euro 2.93. Every customer who switches from the large to the small package would increase total profit (VAT was left out for the sake of simplicity in this case). Besides, this measure would give the store's price image a boost. Only if current sales of the small pack were very high (which is not the case – on the contrary), would the store have to consider other options.

But, interestingly enough, the decision-making partners on the industry and trade side still do not see the connections. At the ECR conference in Amsterdam in 1997, Kraft-Jacobs-Suchard and Rewe, in a joint category management project directed by management consultancy Roland Berger, closely examined the coffee category: with the extremely dubious result of dividing coffee types into the strategies "repeat shopper magnet" (500g packs) and "profit generator" (250g packs).[24] The above example shows that there are problems with profit generation which neither partner – possibly completely unstrategically – has so far perceived.

General consideration of basic issues such as pricing implications – without the burden of columns of figures – is thus just as necessary as developing some imagination about how customers might react to pricing changes. This is how the physicist Binnig's "ignorance theory" translates into food retailing.

Everywhere there are innumerable questions which require creative answers. They should be the central focus of the business. How they are handled determines whether goals will be achieved. Every minor, goal-related question is important and, finally, determines the bottom line. This thinking dominates at ALDI. The others devote themselves too much to cultivating and optimizing their so important planning, information, coordination, communication, marketing, distribution and other systems.

Analyzing masses of data or thinking independently

Never before have managers been able to access such large volumes of data – and rarely have they felt so poorly informed. That is precisely the issue! Thinking and imagination are the essentials! And this works better if a company has no staff departments appointed to think and, most importantly, no staff teams formed to analyze mountains of data. Staff teams keep on producing, whether they are asked to or not. Recently the so-called data warehouse was developed, basically nothing more than an even bigger database. Developments in computer technology make this possible. There are virtually no theoretically conceivable data that cannot not be captured, stored and processed. At Wal-Mart, the largest retailer in the world, data warehousing is already in operation. This system is supposed to be the largest commercial database in the world with a memory of over 100 terabytes. Let's hope Wal-Mart managers do not lose sight of their goals in the long term and their imaginations do not get buried in columns of numbers. Data generate new data, they say at Wal-Mart. Well said! I am convinced that Wal-Mart is not so successful because of its data warehouse, but despite it.

It is advisable for top management to get involved in deciding which statistics the company should produce. Every statistic has to be generated by someone and read by someone, usually by quite a number of people. That costs time and money. Some statistics even lead people to wrong conclusions because their theoretical basis is flawed. It may even be necessary simply to put a ban on the production of certain statistics.

Do not fear the gap. That is another part of the solution. Think independently and try your ideas out. A joint effort will identify what is essential and feasible, and less important factors will automatically drop out. And this approach speeds up work. Nothing is completely without risk. But acting quickly and purposefully is better than spending an infinite amount of time checking anything and everything. That is the reasoning behind the recommendation not to fear the information gap, to be prepared to leave something out and not to feel compelled to examine every detail every time. This requires nerve and a willingness to take risks, responsibly of course.

When there are fewer figures, managers are compelled to reflect and turn their attention to the actual items on sale, the customers and the stores, applying reasonable assumptions about customer behavior. Then, afterwards, it is useful to look at the existing numbers, which should be presented as simply as possible. Each figure then leads on to interesting new questions. You can easily get lost in a world of illusions and dead ends if you believe too firmly in numbers. After all, every number reflects concrete circumstances that have contributed to its development.

Listing or delisting items should be seen in the context of "the purpose of the product range's composition." If these considerations are put on the table first, and a large number of questions are asked about them, a clear picture generally emerges. Only after this should a modest, transparent set of figures be consulted as a final support for the decision. For example sales volumes, revenues, purchase prices. But comparative numbers should always be used as a yardstick.

The detergent example (see section entitled "Shrewd self-restraint on product mix") can also be discussed better initially without any figures. The question is whether the assortment strategy makes it sensible to carry Omo in the 2kg, 3kg or 4kg sizes. Consideration can be given to what is best for the customer. What price advantage can he get? Does a heavier weight pose problems in getting the goods home? What size packs are carried by the competition? Is a small number of items preferred in the product range (for example, because the business is a discounter)?

Which alternatives are available in the range in other brands with similar or different sizes? What strategy promises the best customer response? What does the customer really want?

It is also interesting to ask whether one should study the company's revenues from the item on a monthly (or even weekly), or – in my opinion – preferably quarterly basis. As a rule, trends are not visible within extremely short time periods. Short periods can produce distortions. The company's strategy, in this case the assortment and pricing strategies, should be basic and, therefore, designed for the longer term, avoiding short-term changes and hectic action for action's sake.

Moreover – and this is almost the core point: in comparison to quarterly figures, three sets of monthly figures represent three times the quantity of data. This could then lead to superficial work throughout the whole product range, or once again, assistants, staff functionaries and other employees will be tasked with the analysis. The major advantage at ALDI with the low-data-volume system is that the "bosses" can and must also watch the figures.

A phenomenon which is familiar in nearly all companies in all industries all over the world is drawing up the annual budget, the forecast in numbers of what the company expects in the coming year or years. Some have called budgets toys for chief executive officers. They replace chance with error. Everyone does it. So it has to be right, doesn't it? ALDI gets along without it. Is ALDI making a mistake? This is such a crucial question in every company, and in such stark contrast to ALDI, that a comparison is called for. An article written by the author in *Blick durch die Wirtschaft* (August 5, 1994) briefly discusses the sense and nonsense of budgets:

Excursus: The sense and nonsense of budgets

We have only just presented the many discrepancies between projections and actual figures for the current financial year and painstakingly explained them. We found mistakes and wrong assumptions in the planning and important points were completely forgotten; apart from this, real events have taken a turn which the budget had not expected. And now it is Fall again and that means we have to start drawing up next year's plan. Once again we are groping among uncertainties with no assurance as yet as to how the current year may end. So we juggle our figures, design colorful charts and allow planning and budgeting meetings to keep us from our actual business for weeks at a time.

Of course some planning in the sense of drawing up a budget makes sense, if for example we have to report to supervisory boards about expectations for the coming financial year. But, as a rule, a general set of planning figures covering costs and revenues based on the previous year is sufficient. Likewise, depending on the circumstances of individual businesses, financial, cash flow and personnel planning are needed to some extent.

But how superfluous planning is otherwise, and how much work can be avoided, is shown by the company which nearly everyone respects, admires and fails to understand: ALDI. This food chain store, which is probably the world's most successful, demonstrates how to earn sales volumes greater than 15bn euros without any budgeting.

And yet, instead of concentrating on the essentials, looking after customer interests and making deals, many companies spend large sums with very little to show for it and lose themselves in their fictional worlds of charts and numbers which sooner or later usually vanish into thin air, for good or ill. At ALDI they only work with very few figures, but with key figures, focusing on the most important business processes. And these are not budget figures, but true and actual figures which can be easily established and understood, and which result in transparent conclusions. At ALDI you can see that successful business management has absolutely no need for excessive budget forecasts.

An everyday example from the world of practice: a sales company is subdivided into three sales territories. In June the following deviations from the budget arise:

Area 1 (650 customers)   −5.2 %
Area 2 (750 customers)   −2.1 %
Area 3 (300 customers)   −6.3 %

What conclusions can be reached based on these results? Did area manager 2 work harder in June or had he perhaps made a more conservative forecast? Had the economic climate or the competitive environment been poorly understood? Why these particular discrepancies?

Using a simple comparison of actual figures it is possible to make a breakdown into categories and individual cases showing major deviations from the previous year, previous months or from comparable categories or cases. This would certainly provide explanations because then facts would be compared with facts.

The reasons for the high budget figures can be shown by the following example. Area manager Miller receives praise from his sales manager because he set his future sales high like a "daring entrepreneur." Because he expected this sort of praise, he set his forecast high. Area manager Smith receives criticism because he set his sales forecast low. He is convinced to raise it. He too had expectations regarding how his supervisor would react. The next time plan and actual figures are compared, Miller is criticized because he did not achieve his ambitious goals. Smith, on the other hand, is praised because he surpassed his targets – even after they had be raised.

This is more or less how budget processes work in companies. Frequently they are scientifically "objectified" at enormous effort by analyses and prognoses produced by staff departments. Smith and Miller largely based their figures on the expected reactions of their supervisors. A very wide range of explanations can be used to support budget estimates, but it is only by chance that they occasionally coincide with reality.

Things get interesting when labored attempts are made at meetings to explain deviations from the budget, once more applying the scientific analyses of the staff departments. The many different original assumptions are largely history. The present cannot provide any explanation for a budget error. The most important cause of discrepancies is in the budget itself. Here are a few theses on this subject:

- Budgeting is sensible for the outline information provided to supervisory bodies (supervisory board, advisory board) regarding expectations for the next financial year. A general plan is normally sufficient.
- Budgeting is sensible for limited areas such as finance, cash flow and investments.
- Budgets are not suitable as a yardstick for ongoing control and assessment of business profits.
- Budgets are not suitable for testing the success of business actions or for reviewing employee and department performance.
- Budgets do not justify the amount of time and money put into them.
- The activities for a whole year, with all details, cannot be thought out in advance in the course of a few weeks. This is day-to-day work and not a task requiring a major effort every fall.
- More appropriate are the figures from the previous period (year and month) and comparable figures of similar departments or operations. These compare facts with clearly explainable differences, and not vague and partly random assumptions made under current circumstances which themselves are not always easy to understand.

● Planning departments and their costs are completely superfluous. The responsible line managers can generate the essential analyses with the support of the accounting department more competently than anyone else and, most importantly, draw operational conclusions immediately.

There are excellent companies that operate completely without such plans and the waste of expensive management capacities. They save time and money and are more efficient. They concentrate on the feasible details, bearing in mind the goal of permanent improvement. These companies are – to use a contemporary term – lean. Erich Kästner (1899–1974, a popular German writer) has good advice for all those in love with budgets.

"Forget the plans and get on with improving yourselves."

Decisions on concrete individual cases

One-man decisions about important matters are an absolute rarity at ALDI. Important decisions regarding the organizational structure of the group or on important processes are made after detailed discussions and after possible tests during the general manager meetings, which take place about every six weeks. The same applies to the standard decisions regarding product range and price policy. These are based on detailed thought about each individual item.

Decisions at the general manager meetings are always discussed at great length. As many thoughts and details are included as possible. Decisions are almost never general in nature, but are always made on a concrete case-by-case basis, stemming from the unwritten ALDI culture. ALDI has benefited above all from the fact that no generally valid rules were established as is the practice at many other companies. ALDI is in a position to study individual cases, because the company is simply structured and, what's more, the limited product range makes it possible to consider every individual article.

Supermarket companies, for example, establish rules that say they will list brand leaders in every case, or on principle. At the same time, an item is selected which can compete with the low prices of, say, ALDI. These two are then rounded off by a medium-range priced item, for example the second-place or third-place national brand.

Another rule might be to hold all prices 5 percent below those of certain competitors or of the cheapest competitor, or never to sell under the purchase price. Such rules are established as principles for the whole product range. Every employee in purchasing or sales then knows for sure what the guidelines are. They think that "those above" have to tell "those below" what they have to be guided by.

But what are the real problems of such rules? Are they sufficiently thought out? Do they apply to every individual case? Do they fit every eventuality or every special situation?

All companies should design their organizations so that individual cases, individual items, individual customers, individual production processes, individual employees can be considered. This is possible by means of decentralization and delegation. Too many general rules can too easily be faulty and, thus, dangerous.

Tom Peters is obsessed with the limitless potential of retailing. He, too, sees that they frequently give something away. What he likes best about retailing is that it is not exposed to management interference and that the stores are completely self-managing and sovereign bodies. The guru of management know-how is seriously mistaken here, and underestimates the powerful effect of rules. They act as management's remote control of the product range and price variables which are so decisive in retailing. The "sovereign" in the store only has the advantage that his bosses are not constantly breathing down his neck.

The administrative board

The administrative board as the highest decision-making authority in the ALDI Group (formally in each individual ALDI company) has the authority and power to make any issue a matter of its own concern. Like virtually every highest body in every company, it can override any valid regulation or any previously accepted practice. This is also the litmus test of ALDI and its culture and organization, as praised in this book.

Today, the administrative board, in addition to its chairman Theo Albrecht and his sons Theo Jr. and Berthold, consists of three other former ALDI general managers. The members of the administrative board are self-employed, i.e. not employees of a holding company or a specific company. As already mentioned, this arrangement allows the organization to avoid the structure of a group of affiliated companies with its various disadvantages. The administrative board members act as supervisory board members in the individual ALDI companies. They have control functions, but also a decision-making role and right of veto.

The approach of the board to its work is heavily influenced by the individual members and, of course, especially by Theo Albrecht. He loves details so that long discussions can also take place about less important questions. He fears that the best solutions will not always be found or that mistakes are being made, so that there is always the tendency to continue to fine-tune checking procedures and regulations to iron out every last wrinkle. This approach is based on a more skeptical than trust-based understanding of human nature. Still, with the help of the delegation principle, appropriate and harmonious working methods have been ensured so far.

What authority does the owner have?

My subjective view will reflect how I experienced Theo Albrecht. These comments are important for an understanding of the company because the entrepreneurs Karl and Theo Albrecht have left the strongest mark on their group of individual companies.

It is known that the working methods of Karl Albrecht and Theo Albrecht are very distinct from one another. Theo Albrecht is devoted to details, Karl Albrecht is a loyal defender of traditional principles. Karl Albrecht withdrew from day-to-day business several years ago, Theo Albrecht, at 79, is still very active today. This too shows good sense of the brothers' separation in the early 1960s.

His personality makes it is very difficult for Theo Albrecht to let go of the business. He was always a very cautious man and he needs to feel that he is in control. A person is most likely to have this feeling, of course, if he comes into work early in the morning. He has expanded this control by making his two sons, Theo Jr. and Berthold, members of the administrative board.

The interesting question arises of how ALDI (ALDI North in this case) could be successfully managed for so many years considering the owner's style of leadership, based on mistrust? This seems especially remarkable if you consider the company's virtues which are described in such great detail above. The great advantage and the good fortune of the group was the uncompromising decentralization and delegation of areas of responsibility, which of course Theo Albrecht also supported. Thus the general managers of the ALDI companies could run their business operations with relatively little interference and achieve best practices within the scope of their authority.

Theo Albrecht's direct influence was restricted almost exclusively to the administrative board which, in turn, acted as a protective levee for the ALDI companies. Basically, Theo Albrecht was not a genuine supporter of uncompromising delegation principles by nature. For this he would have needed a more positive view of people, a necessary component of trust. His attitude might have been destructive without the filter of the administrative board. However, Theo Albrecht has always been a reliable and agreeable partner. Friendly, never loud or unrestrained. He is the fatherly chairman of the administrative board, more advisor than critic.

The major achievement of the owners is and remains the great oak that arose from their original little acorns. Later the influence of professional managers became important, at ALDI North initially Ekkehard Asbeck, later Otto Hübner together with myself; at ALDI South Horst Steinfeld and Ulrich Wolters. They contributed substantially to the shaping of the organization and then, though together with Karl and Theo Albrecht, ensured that the company stuck to its basic principles. The ALDI managers are nearly completely unknown in public because ALDI in general avoids any public appearances. Who knows Dr. Ulrich Wolters? Not long ago, Erivan Haub, the owner of Tengelmann and the A&P Group, named him in response to a survey as the most important German manager of the past decade. Erivan Haub is right.

Theo Albrecht's fondness for details and the solid expertise which often comes along with that enabled him to set good examples. In his exclusive position as owner, however, he was never really required to exercise normal supervisory or general manager functions. This is probably true of most company owners. That also makes it difficult and nearly impossible to assess their leadership abilities. The conspicuous special features, the typical characteristics are more likely to be known. In Theo Albrecht's case these are undoubtedly the exaggerated attention to detail and his "healthy" skepticism, coupled with a fear of losses in business and in private life. When he stayed in a hotel his first act after taking his room was always to check where the escape route was in case of emergency. A sensible act which reflected his extreme caution.

After all, not everything was entirely to the benefit of the company. The administrative board which Theo Albrecht chairs became overly concerned with the personal special issues that were of such interest to him. But of course the owner expects that this will be tolerated and accepted. In my professional experience it is also typical that the people at the very top are often the kind who tend to make themselves the measure of all things.

For example, the chairman of the administrative board plans the janitor's apartment for a new ALDI company and thinks over how the bedroom could be designed and decorated. He asks a member of the administrative board to look into the question of whether thin or thick photocopies are better or more economical. The same administrative board member is also expected to find out how the desks in the telephone exchange would be best arranged. These sort of things can also intensely frustrate managers who love efficiency and responsibility.

But it was an organizationally important and successful decision to have each ALDI company run by only one general manager, i.e. not to have any multi-headed management teams. If the general manager was the right person it was fine, if he was the wrong person, it was possible to replace him or look into how his leadership could be improved. This meant that problems such as those the administrative board had with itself could be avoided in the course of business operations.

Special features of the ALDI organization

Eight years after *In Search of Excellence*, Tom Peters summarized his insights as follows:[25]

> *"The eight basic principles of successful companies identified*
> *eight years ago can actually be concentrated into one:*
> *decentralization and autonomy."*
> Tom Peters

The secret of success is that decentralization turns many employees into entrepreneurs inside the enterprise, intrapreneurs. I consider this principle of leadership and organization to be the dazzling recipe for success at the ALDI organization.

What is fundamentally different at ALDI in terms of leadership and organization? Only those special ALDI characteristics which are sharply unconventional are summarized opposite:

What are the special characteristics of ALDI organization and leadership?

Clear objectives
Simple and understandable for everyone.

Rigorous decentralization and delegation
That means: delegate as much as possible. But the decisive point is rigorous implementation.

Systematic checks
For all delegated tasks there is a good control system.

Few management papers/statistics
Courage to think is developed, creativity applied independent of figures.

No staff functions
All special tasks are handled by line managers.

No budgets
Intelligent comparisons drawn from actual figures are the yardstick for all assessments.

Top management to the front line
Top managers must feel and see how customers experience the company

---

In addition to these, ALDI has developed many techniques to resolve details which are not included in this book.

The essential point is always implementation. This is what shows how difficult understanding and comprehension is in individual cases, especially for the many employees who have to handle the practical side of implementation.

In my day-to-day work in Germany, but mostly in my work in Italy and Turkey, a series of very tangible examples showed me how difficult implementation is. Narrow-mindedness and a lack of imagination due to different personal backgrounds frequently dominate. One top manager who had held top executive positions for many years in the branded goods industry had incredible difficulties understanding what admittedly appeared to be the simple system of a hard discounter. It was as if the pilot of an auto-piloted Airbus was being expected to make a donkey gallop. In his large, international company, some things had been functioning for many years according to certain rules. No matter how things were going, he did not need to look after it. Somehow things worked. Such managers become increasingly accustomed to living with the bureaucracy of their companies. It is difficult for them to get involved again directly with customer and market-related matters or to take an interest in what their employees really need in order to be able to work successfully.

Part 3
Business principles

The five principles of the ALDI sales strategy

When successful companies are studied, the pivotal question that repeatedly arises is: what is really behind their market leadership? Klaus Wiegandt, former CEO at Metro-Holding, specifies three success factors which he has identified in the course of analyzing successful companies in Europe and the United States and which were to play a role in the restructuring of Metro:

- Monostructure – only one type of sales format
- Rigor and an obsession with details
- No foreign engagements until the company is firmly in place at home.

It is apparent that Wiegandt's analysis had one particular company in mind. ALDI is the prototype of the successful company when judged by these criteria.

The American management consultants Michael Treacy and Fred Wiersema[26] have attributed "operational leadership" to ALDI and the computer maker Dell. By operational leadership they mean excellence in cost and organization. The operational dimension, the excellent implementation of the business ideas, is their special achievement. The primary consideration in this context is not the uniqueness of the business idea. Operational leadership – especially cost leadership – is thus the decisive prerequisite for price leadership. Although a company like ALDI is unthinkable without the idea of a limited product range, nevertheless, without its clear cost leadership in nearly all operational areas, ALDI's market leadership is unimaginable.

It is notable that many important companies – such as Norma or Lidl in Germany – are quite openly attempting to imitate ALDI principles. Or they talk about how they have taken ALDI as the model for their industry, as have Möbel Roller (one of the largest German furniture retailers), Vobis (a computer retailer) and the advertising agency White Lion. These companies have taken their cue from ALDI's obvious business principles: limited product range (not carrying every item or offering every service), good quality, and price leadership. These basic ideas normally also lead to the associated best operational performance for the imitators, too.

Companies should be capable of developing their own business principles in line with their own cultures. ALDI has succeeded in doing this. Although ALDI always kept an eye on the competition, the competition was never a source of "benchmarks" for ALDI's own practice. ALDI has always set its own course.

The ALDI business principles, where they are relevant to sales strategy, i.e. market image, can be summarized in five points:

- a limited product range,
- goods which reflect basic consumer needs,
- easily handled goods in terms of operational requirements,
- best possible qualities – measured against leading brands,
- the lowest possible retail prices.

The lowest prices anywhere

The company's inbuilt basic principle is to sell products at the lowest prices possible. It was never a goal to get the highest possible prices allowed by the competitive environment. This paid off in terms of the company's standing in the eyes of the customers: "ALDI's prices are incredibly reasonable for us consumers" a customer said in the LZ consumer panel,[27] an experience-sharing discussion held at regular intervals on various subjects related to food shopping by *Lebensmittel-Zeitung*. It is said that ALDI shoppers belong to one of two groups: those who have to budget, and those who are capable of budgeting.

Publications have repeatedly supported ALDI. The cookbook *ALDIdente* by Astrid Paprotta and Regina Schneider, is the latest proof of this. A quarter of a century earlier Frank Görtz, in his book *The Smart Shopper's Guide to Saving Money* (*Der Einkaufsführer – Ein Ratgeber zum Geldsparen* published in 1974) compared a shopping basket of 61 products and came to the conclusion: "All 61 items in the basket were cheaper at ALDI." Much cheaper, as the overall comparison shows:

ALDI	euro 110.75
Normal supermarket	euro 171.50

Erwin Conradi, former chairman of Metro's supervisory board, estimated the importance of low prices in clear terms in an interview with the weekly German newspaper Die Zeit – provocatively in view of the rising notion of establishing ambiences for shopping:

"The customer gets his biggest kick from finding a good price, and he still feels good about it after he gets home."

In a certain region of the ALDI group a 1983/1984 price comparison of 120 items for the main hypermarkets which pursued aggressive pricing as their strategy showed the following results:

	Same price as ALDI	Cheaper than ALDI	More expensive than ALDI
Marktkauf AVA Bielefeld	45%	2%	53%
Realkauf Schaper/Asko Hannover	30%	4%	66%
Regional market leaders	15%	2%	83%

A current shopping basket comparison that I carried out in Hamburg in early May 2000 included a normal supermarket, known for its good product range and quality merchandise (Spar, Eppendorfer Landstraße), as well as ALDI's toughest competitor in the German market (Lidl, Hammer Landstraße). The results are listed below.

Shopping basket comparison, May 2000 – DM

Item	ALDI	Lidl	Spar
Long-life milk, 1 liter	0.95	0.95	1.19
Flour type 405 1kg	0.45	0.45	0.59
Granulated sugar 1kg	1.69	1.69	1.79
Whole grain rolled oats 500g	0.49	0.49	0.99
Whole grain crisp bread 250g	0.69	0.69	2.29
Whole grain sliced bread 500g	0.95	0.79	1.99
Butter 250g	1.69	1.69	1.99
Sunflower oil margarine 500g	0.99	0.99	1.39
Low-fat quark 500g	0.99	0.99	1.39
Natural yogurt 150g	0.25	0.25	0.39
Smoked salmon 200g	4.29	4.29	6.65
Eggs pack of 10, large	1.09	1.09	2.99
Frozen creamed spinach 450g	0.89	0.89	0.99
Carrots 1kg	1.79	1.99	2.99
New potatoes 2.5kg	2.99	3.31	3.99
Bananas 1kg	1.79	1.88	2.99
Onions 2kg	2.39	2.98	3.98
Mixed sweet peppers 500g	3.59	3.05	6.30
Coffee "Gold" quality 500g	5.79	5.29	8.99
Evaporated milk 10% 340g	0.79	0.79	1.49
Coffee filters 100 sheets size 4	0.99	0.99	1.19

Orange juice 0.75 liter	1.39	1.39	1.99
Carrot juice 0.33 liter	0.79	0.65	1.79
Beer 0.5 liter can	0.59	0.59	0.79
Vodka 0.7 liter (37.5%)	8.98	8.98	9.99
Brandy 0.7 liter (36%)	8.98	8.98	9.99
Sour cherry preserves 450g	1.59	1.59	1.79
Plum compote 450g	3.04	1.49	1.79
Honey 500g	2.29	2.29	3.99
Nut-nougat spread 400g	1.59	1.59	1.79
Prince cookies bag 500g	1.39	1.39	1.79
Hazelnut chocolate 100g	0.49	0.49	1.19
Hazelnuts shelled 200g	1.99	1.79	1.49
Morellos (jarred cherries) 720ml	2.60	2.60	3.00
Silesian pickles 580ml	1.00	1.00	2.40
Lentil stew 800ml	1.60	1.90	2.00
Olive oil cold pressed 750ml	4.30	4.30	9.00
Laundry detergent 1.5kg	4.98	4.98	5.00
Shampoo 500ml	1.60	1.60	3.70
Panty-liners 45 pads	2.30	4.46	3.20
Toothpaste 125ml	1.00	1.00	1.30
Aluminum foil 30 cm/30 m	2.30	2.30	3.00
Dog food 850ml	1.10	1.10	1.30
Total	DM 91.42	DM 91.99	DM 128.83
Price index	100.00	100.62	140.05

* There were two items which Lidl did not carry. Variant quantities were adjusted in individual cases to match ALDI quantities. In order to make it easier to compare the shopping basket as a whole, a fictional price was assumed for these items, based on the average price difference in relation to ALDI of 0.62%.

The comparison took the cheapest products sold by ALDI's competitors. These were either brand names or the competitor's private labels. Experience has shown that one can assume that ALDI products are at least as good as the branded products – in this sampling the least expensive ones – but in general significantly better than the competitor's private-label lines.

Apparently, in the face of stiff competition, ALDI rarely succeeds any more in being substantially cheaper than its closest competitor Lidl. The latter clearly uses ALDI as a yardstick when setting prices. Lidl is increasingly more competitive thanks to their private labels. A price comparison including the same items some 20 months earlier showed Lidl to be still nearly 7 percent more expensive than ALDI. But even Sparmarkt was able to reduce the price gap between itself and ALDI in the same time period from 55 to 41 percent. At the same time Spar increased the share of private label products on its shelves.

For the comparison with the Spar supermarket chain which carries primarily brand names, individual items at Spar may indeed be better quality than those at ALDI. Experience – also reflected by the results of the German consumer goods test institute, Stiftung Warentest – shows, however, that ALDI offers the better quality in nearly all cases, frequently even better than that of the brand names.

Regarding the higher prices at Spar, it should be noted that they have a different sales concept from the discounters. The wide product range, the large fresh food sections and, last but not least, their more expensive locations make a different price strategy essential. But the market is still very popular, and I also shop there regularly. Companies must repeatedly ask themselves: "Why should the customer shop in my store?" And the reasons are different for Spar and ALDI.

No one disputes the fact that ALDI sets prices in the food retail trade. The market price is determined by ALDI, at least the lower key value.

Formerly, ALDI rarely took its cue for price changes from competitors' prices, they set the prices themselves. If the purchase price drops, ALDI almost automatically lowers its sales price. ALDI achieves its best values for prices by cost-cutting in all areas – with the exception of wages and salaries which generally are among the highest but, due to the high productivity of staff, nevertheless generate the lowest personnel costs. Price competition in Germany and Europe has taken on a new quality since the market entry of the US giant Wal-Mart. At the moment Wal-Mart is still re-examining its product range and pricing strategies. In late May 1999, the consumer had to pay some 20 percent more in the former Wertkauf (now Wal-Mart) market in Hamburg-Oststeinbek than at ALDI for the above shopping basket. Especially in the area of private labels, Wal-Mart still has some way to go to catch up with ALDI. But it won't be long.

Price wars

Today, ALDI is increasingly compelled to demonstrate its price leadership. This leads on occasion to genuine price wars between the leading discounters – often joined by the large hypermarkets. In the struggle for market shares there is only one weapon in discounting: the price. In November 1994 the German trade magazine *Lebensmittel-Zeitung* reported on a "price war started by ALDI." According to reports, ALDI wanted to lower the prices on half of its products and sacrifice roughly 250 million euros in earnings. ALDI's lower price on long-life milk alone was set to cost the Rewe group 12.5 million euros in earnings. In October 1997 the *Lebensmittel-Zeitung* reported on drastic price cuts of up to 15% on margarine and oil products under the headline "ALDI slams the compeitition."[28] Within just one week all the competitors reduced prices to match. Of course, ALDI's offensive was directed once again at its closest rivals, Lidl and Penny.

For some years ALDI has been struggling with Lidl's major expansion efforts and aggressive price strategies. This is what lies behind such "price wars." The price is the sole strong argument with which Lidl can attempt to grab market share from ALDI. The above price comparison between ALDI and Lidl shows that ALDI cannot be entirely happy with what is happening in the market.

In May 1997, there was a price war between Penny and Lidl. Both companies have their own particular problems to struggle with. Lidl is grappling with its incredibly fast-paced expansion across Europe. Not all the locations deliver the expected, or even the necessary results. Penny, which has been around for some time now, has been seeking a new position as a hard discounter for years after having gone very "soft" earlier.

Considering the price war, the *Lebensmittel-Zeitung* of 16 May 1997 then expected that ALDI would "strike back without mercy." What will happen? It is true that ALDI cannot look on at these battles unmoved. But without any particular problems of its own, ALDI is in a position to keep up with pace of developments over many years without having to draw on its existing capital. The profit margin is large enough that ALDI can afford to make further price cuts if need be. But if ALDI reacts, then the company will be offering much lower prices than the others. That is a matter of the company's values. Reactions can therefore be expected – to the benefit of the consumers, at the expense of the retailers' profits.

Quality is more important than anything else – private label strategy

One of the decisive success factors, aside from the principle of the lowest possible prices, is quality and – associated with this – a rigorous private label strategy. Around 95 percent of all the items on ALDI's shelves are private label, but they are often made by well-known branded goods manufacturers such as Bahlsen, De Beukelaer, Blendax, Trumpf, Nestlé or Unilever. No one else has pursued this policy so rigorously.

The success of this strategy was supported to a significant extent by the results of the consumer testing laboratory *Stiftung Warentest* which frequently gave ALDI private label products better ratings than the brand name products – with generally drastic price differences. Suppliers know that they face serious sanctions if their items show poor results. And even a "satisfactory" is normally regarded as poor. But ALDI uses the opportunity to respond with moderation to such quality shortcomings: if an item is only rated "satisfactory," a supplier who previously supplied perhaps six ALDI distribution centers may initially have two distribution centers cut from his list until he has improved the quality of his products. If the products receive a lower rating than that, however, the item is generally de-listed immediately.

Suppliers know the ALDI quality requirements. They have to meet them. The best raw materials and excellent processing are expected. Since the suppliers do not have long-term contracts, ALDI can also immediately terminate business relationships without the need for interminable legal wrangling – frequently after an interim period so that existing packaging can be used up. Nevertheless, ALDI has rarely taken such tough action that a supplier's existence was endangered. This is also the reason why ALDI is not interested in making suppliers dependent on its order quantities. Often, an additional supplier is brought into the delivery process at an early stage.

In the case of Schiesser, at that time one of the largest bread makers in Germany, which filed for bankruptcy in mid-1997, ALDI remained very patient in response to increasing incidents involving quality-related and delivery problems. But in the end ALDI was compelled to act so as not to endanger its reputation with its own customers. In general the reasons for such faults in suppliers can be found exclusively in their own companies and in their poor management, and have nothing to do with ALDI's low sales prices.

Several examples from the tests carried out by *Stiftung Warentest* are shown in the next table. Price comparisons are based as a rule on specific standardized quantities, such as 100ml, or on a unit of consumption, such as one load of laundry. The results relate to ALDI North and ALDI

South, which very frequently have the same prices and, usually, the same quality standard.

In recent years *Stiftung Warentest* has tested fewer groceries than it used to. Today, only taste and recipe studies are carried out and described without any final overall judgment. Here too, ALDI is nearly always awarded the rating of "very good" in terms of quality and price.

Test results of the Stiftung Warentest

Item	Number of tested items — Very good	Good	Poorer	Rating for ALDI	Prices Range (units)	ALDI Price (DM)
1996						
Clear apple juice	5	12	3	Good	1.10–2.25	1.32
Natural apple juice	2	7	2	Poor *(ALDI North) – item de-listed*		
Fish sticks	2	7	7	Very good	0.42–1.11	0.42
Instant chocolate	1	16	3	Good	0.35–0.80	0.35
Body lotion	0	8	1	Good	0.05–0.60	0.05
Sun protection (cream) SPF 8–12	9	2	3	Very good	3.98–97.50	3.98
Sun protection (milk) SPF 6–8	10	3	1	Very good	0.92–9.95	0.92
Dishwasher detergent	0	4	10	Poor *(ALDI North) – item de-listed* Satisfactory *(ALDI South)*		
1995						
Frozen chicken	0	5	6	Good	0.62–1.66	0.62
Frozen dinner	0	1	9	Satisfactory	0.55–1.58	0.55
Fish sticks frozen	2	7	7	Very good	0.42–1.11	0.42
Detergent for delicates	0	11	0	Good	0.19–1.05	0.19
1994						
Laundry detergent	0	16	0	Good	0.23–0.62	0.24/0.27
Skin cream	0	4	7	Satisfactory	1.00–8.00	1.00
Native olive oil	3	12	5	Very good	6.12–49.80	6.12
Washing-up liquid	0	10	6	Good	0.52–3.00	0.52
Orange juice	2	13	5	Good	0.89–4.27	0.89
Shower gel	0	16	0	Good	0.33–4.49	0.33
Shampoo	0	14	0	Good	0.32–10.00	0.32
Skin cream	0	1	5	Satisfactory	1.00–8.00	1.00

1993						
Scouring powder	0	11	2	Good	0.20–0.77	0.20
All-purpose cleaner	0	12	0	Good	0.01–0.41	0.05
Laundry detergent						
for colors	0	4	1	Good	0.31–0.63	0.34
Shower gel	0	18	1	Good	0.33–4.70	0.33
1992						
Laundry detergent	0	16	0	Good	0.33–0.72	0.33
Shampoo	0	14	2	Good	0.60–4.73	0.80
Skincare lotion	0	14	2	Good	0.60–9.95	0.72
Dishwasher powder	0	0	8	Satisfactory	0.08–0.24	0.08
1990						
Pasta	5	0	2	Very good	0.69–1.79	0.69
Dishwashing detergent	0	6	21	Satisfactory	0.20–0.70	0.20
Dog food dry	0	11	2	Good	0.12–0.26	0.16
Dog food canned	0	13	4	Good	0.39–2.33	0.39

ALDI's rigorous quality strategy also led to impressive test results from the IGD Europanel for Germany. A survey of the image of private labels found that 85 percent of those questioned thought that private labels were cheaper; 90 percent estimated that private labels and branded goods were equivalent in terms of quality; confidence in the product was also the same at 84 percent. The findings of this survey of German consumers were most likely determined by their exposure to ALDI.

The importance of private labels became especially clear when the ALDI private label laundry detergent, Tandil, achieved for a time a market share of 25 percent in the trade journals. Every consumer knows the famous detergent names Persil, Omo, Ariel, Weißer Riese which are promoted in enormous advertising campaigns and can be found in nearly every shop. I believe one important explanation for the success of private labels is the considerable commitment of retailers and their employees in pushing their own label. Brand names have a comparatively "anonymous" standing.

The No. 1 in coffee

The strength of ALDI's private labels is even more evident in the case of coffee than it is for laundry detergent. In Germany no coffee gets a better rating than Albrecht Gold. Tchibo and Jacobs were always given poorer ratings during internal tests. Regarding roasted coffee, an extremely important item in Germany, Klaus Jacobs, quoted in the German weekly business magazine *Wirtschaftswoche*, stated: "Our number one competitor is clearly ALDI." ALDI could hardly have received a higher compliment. Jacobs coffee is sold in every shop, every convenience store and at every service station across Germany, while ALDI coffee is merely sold in 3,000 stores. But after Germany's re-unification, and after Eduscho had been taken over by Tchibo (these were previously rival specialized coffee retailers with similar formats), market shares have shifted considerably, so that ALDI should now be a clear third. In the mid-1980s the market looked like this:

Market shares 1985

Tchibo	18.9%
Jacobs	18.5%
ALDI	18.2%
Eduscho	14.2%
Melitta	4.1%

In 1994 newspaper reports stated that Jacobs had conceded its market leadership in the states of the former West Germany to ALDI:

Market shares in the former West Germany 1994

ALDI	19%
Jacobs	14%

The whole industry – apart from ALDI and Melitta – had to face painful volume losses in 1994.[29]

	Market shares 1994 former West and East Germany	% change from 1993	Market shares 1997
Jacobs	21.8%	−12.0	30%
Tchibo	15.5%	−9.7	20%
ALDI	14.4%	+7.9	13%
Eduscho	10.8%	−9.4	11%
Melitta	9.7%	+6.8	12%

The reader should take note: all other coffee brands are sold everywhere, but the ALDI brands are only sold in their own stores. It is also worth noting that the German anti-trust office finally approved the merger in

1997 of Tchibo and Eduscho, which together account for 30 percent of the German market, because it would not give them a "dominant market share." The closet market leader, in the office's opinion, was ALDI, which was "already regulating prices."[30]

Coffee tests were part of the after lunch ritual at the ALDI head-quarters in Essen. Administrative board members and the chief purchasing officer met for a blind coffee test, coupled with an exchange of ideas related to any aspect of ALDI. You could call them C&C rounds: coffee and communication.

The list of successful private labels can be extended to other product categories: turnover of ALDI private labels Regent (ALDI North) and Diplomat (ALDI South) brandy, amounting to roughly 50 million euros, is probably about as high as that of the strong national brand Asbach, which can be bought nearly anywhere in Germany. The 20 million euros in sales of Cognacs Rayon (ALDI North) and Royal (ALDI South) make these brands nearly as successful as Remy Martin. One final example: cigarettes. The private labels "Tobacco House Nr. 7" and "Boston" are more than the sales of all other brands in ALDI stores.

Quality-conscious consumers

Private labels require confident, knowledgeable consumers: quality and price as rational arguments against the irrational "brand" idea. Or, as Papprotta and Schneider put it: ALDI customers do not need labels to boost their feelings of personal adequacy. For example, ALDI carried the beer Radeberger Pils, an import from the former East Germany, more than twenty years ago – and today it is also a widely known beer in Germany's western states. The customers appreciated the quality back then, supported of course by ALDI's own special pricing strategy.

Consumers are extremely capable of judging quality themselves, and making themselves independent of brand advertising campaigns. Eileen Shapiro describes in her book *Fad Surfing in the Boardroom* the transition from the age of brand loyalty to the age of product value. The success of ALDI private labels clearly supports these ideas: product value has the priority.

Virtually all the important producers are increasingly manufacturing private labels or white labels. Private labels are already estimated to account for nearly 40 percent of the German market – if genuine ALDI figures were included, this share would probably be even significantly higher. All the statistics and surveys of market changes in Europe show strong growth in private labels. And the stronger the concentration – and thus company size – in retailing is, the faster private labels will grow. For some manufacturers this has meant a great opportunity for some years, but also a problem for the brand name producers who invested heavily in research and development and would like to get a return on their investment by charging high prices. But white labels can achieve higher profit contributions, if you take into account the considerable advertising outlays and substantial promotional costs which burden branded goods.

Many manufacturers produce white labels for nearly all discounters and food chains. Bauer yogurt is available as a private label at Rewe (Penny, Minimal, Toom, HL), at Tengelmann (Plus, Ledi), at Lidl (discounters and hypermarkets) and at Metro (C+C, Real supermarkets). In the future one of the major tasks of retailers and manufacturers will be to give these products competitive differentiation, especially in terms of quality. Even a private label product must be more than just a name.

There are two decisive factors behind ALDI's successful quality policy. Quality standards of items are based on leading branded products. As a principle, differences in the purchase prices of different qualities are not a factor in the decision-making process. A higher purchase price is accepted for higher quality.

Rigorous quality control

Another decisive point for ALDI's success is rigorous quality control. In every ALDI company it is customary for the senior management based at headquarters to meet, usually around lunch-time, for quality testing. Blind tastings of ALDI's private labels and the leading brand labels take place every day.

How often have I seen employees – sometimes also guests or job applicants who had just come out of an interview – mistaken in identifying products. The assumption seems to be widespread that we tend to "drink labels" or "smoke cigar brands." I have met people who claimed they would be able to identify the original Coca-Cola among hundreds of products. But during the quality test at ALDI headquarters they then ranked their Coca-Cola as number 2 or 3, and put ALDI's own brand in first place. I will never forget a supplier of the German spirit Korn who maintained he could smell his product "through the bottle." During the test he ranked his product as number 3. The expert gave first place to

ALDI, and second place to a vodka(!), which the expert had not noticed was a vodka. Like little children we spent many a half hour tasting the Nutella chocolate spread with the private label and other brands. You really sometimes have to taste five or six times before you can judge with any degree of reliability. Those were the benchmarks.

Moreover, purchasing and the incoming goods department have obligations to meet in each of the over 60 distribution centers. These include sensory inspections, laboratory analyses – naturally performed by independent laboratories – as well as weight tests or even counting the number of sheets on toilet paper rolls to determine whether there are really 200 as claimed. Relevant records are kept of all the checks.

Several examples:

- Samples are taken of every shipment of canned fruit, vegetable and fish.
- Samples are also taken of each shipment received and individual units weighed.
- Each week at least two types of sausages or cold cuts are checked.
- Each paper product is tested at least once monthly.
- Eggs are submitted to weight and quality controls each time a shipment is received according to special, detailed rules.
- General weight checks take place on a daily basis, for some items this involves selecting a certain number of samples.
- As part of the daily checks ten items are taken out of the distribution center's inventory.
- Each purchaser carries out quality comparisons with competitive items within his category.

There is hardly a competitor of ALDI who carries out such extensive quality controls, at least in my professional experience I have yet to find one. This extensive and complicated control system is the basis of the confidence that ALDI itself and its customers can have in the quality of the products. This is how private labels generate confidence in retailers. This is also how to create greater independence from suppliers.

Of course, ALDI's terms of purchase commit its suppliers to certain warranties. For example: "The supplier gives assurance that he has designed the manufacturing process in such a manner, above and beyond careful selection and supervision of his staff, that the possibility of any unintended adulterations is ruled out, or at least of the sale of adulterated or misleadingly designated goods." Or: "The supplier will submit a test report, written by an independent testing laboratory, no later than one month after the first delivery."

When it comes to freshness, ALDI can hardly be beat. Its rapid turnover makes it practically impossible for competitors to offer fresher wares. This is especially true for packaged bread: daily delivery and quick sales are the reasons. Of course this does not protect ALDI from some prejudices that it has to live with. The *Lebensmittel Zeitung* quoted one customer during one of its "consumer surveys" who said, "the eggs at ALDI are not as fresh." There is no doubt whatever that the exact opposite is true. Nowhere are they fresher. Nowhere are eggs tested more intensively for freshness and quality – every single time there is a delivery. Here too, the immense advantages of the narrow product range become apparent; it enables ALDI to pay a great deal of attention to controlling the quality and freshness of each individual item.

Another side of implementing ALDI's quality principle is that the branch managers are not given the authority to reject customer returns. Returns are handled extraordinarily generously. In really extreme cases the branch manager must notify his supervisor, the district manager, and ask him to decide. Unlike what many would like to think, ALDI has discovered that customers rarely abuse this generosity.

Reliable, uniformly perfect quality was and remains decisive for ALDI's success – more importantly than any specific distribution system. A distribution system can be watched, analyzed and copied. Such a fanatic and no-compromise quality policy, however, requires a specific corporate culture and this requires people who think, feel and act accordingly.

600 items define the company

ALDI's success is the success of voluntary self-control. For decades ALDI North kept its product range down to 600 items. At present this figure has probably grown to 700. ALDI South today sells 650 items.

Formerly, ALDI only sold so-called dry goods. Refrigeration or special handling were not necessary. Today, the equipment and logistics necessary for refrigerated and frozen goods present no problems. The personnel do not require any special background knowledge about ALDI products either. But, for this reason, there will be no place for meat on ALDI shelves in the future either. Fruit and vegetables can now be successfully handled with some restrictions.

At ALDI North the items break down as follows:

570	Dry goods delivered from distribution centers
70	Refrigerated products (dairy, sausage, cold cuts) delivered from distribution centers
35	Frozen foods, including ice cream, delivered directly by the suppliers
10	Bread and other baked goods, delivered directly by the suppliers
15	ALDI current specials (non-food)
700	

Six hundred items are controllable. Each item is an individual and can be treated as such by everyone all the way up to the top management. "People know" each individual item personally when there are only 600. When that figure rises to 700 – formerly 750 at Aldi North – this gets somewhat more difficult.

But should not companies selling thousands of items be able to do the same thing, at least to some extent? At the end of the day, the customer only buys one or his specific item. How many sisters, brothers and other relatives this one item has is of no concern to him. He never buys the whole merchandise category of jellies, he just buys one, for example "small jar of low-sugar, cherry jelly." But this is one of the biggest problems for all of ALDI's competitors. Even starting from 2000, and certainly when the range goes up to 20,000 items, managers at other retailers must resort to generalized methods of quality assurance and product range management. But there are solutions.

One solution is to delegate decision-making authority on questions related to product range and pricing to the branches within an explicit set of guidelines. Today some retailers are attempting just this – but only half-heartedly. Even for their independent merchants with whom they have cooperative or cooperation-type agreements, the Rewe headquarters word their agreements to enable them to exercise influence on the product ranges in the stores. But this should be the sole decision of the merchant in the field. Rewe calls this form of influence its "partnership model." Though such a policy in my opinion is not clever, it is nevertheless understandable if you consider how the retail trade is weighted in favor of purchasing.

In an article which appeared in the *Lebensmittel-Zeitung* in 1997 with the title "New freedom for supermarket managers," Uwe Rosmanith discusses the questions which Rewe faced as representative of the situation at many other companies. To what extent does the local entrepreneur, with his access to price and assortment, counteract the very strategy which most large retailers initiated at headquarters? In conjunction with the relevant performance incentives to the industry and the goal of achieving the best purchase price by bundling, there are good reasons why assortment procurement and management have been centralized.

The customer is not factored into this argument at all, and the tasty notion of "customer orientation" shrinks to mere lip service. The one and only concern here is negotiating further tenths of a percent from the manufacturer. And the outlets reflect this situation: the product ranges in retail stores frequently give the impression that the shelves are suppliers' trade fair booths.

In my practical experience, characterized by the principles of delegation, I came up with a new solution to the problem of "How can I manage 6,000 items?" A sales assistant in one store once called it the "toothpaste philosophy."

The toothpaste philosophy

The "toothpaste philosophy" means that many sales assistants and the category managers in the stores (not the store managers) are given a small merchandise category to manage. This sales assistant is the contact for the purchasing department and purchasing must not make any product range decisions without consulting her.

And what is exactly her task? She considers whether her category is optimally structured in terms of the company's defined general guidelines. She thinks about whether the package sizes are appropriate, whether individual items can be de-listed, whether important items are missing. She can experiment, try out various placements, and possibly even make pricing decisions. She also visits competitors to see how they are doing things. In this way she becomes the company's expert and her know-how gives her a headstart over every purchaser so that she is in a position to help him. She can approach her supervisor, the store manager or her colleagues as contact and advisors.

And why not? The main objection from traditionalists will always be. "She simply cannot do it." Wrong! She can. There are not many people, by the way, who recognize that food retailing is an ideal business for this kind of approach because these assistants, who are usually women, have a degree of experience which makes them "experts" in these fields. These employees shop on a daily basis, make meals for their families and are, in any case, themselves consumers.

So I can only plead: show some courage in retailing! Leave the beaten paths behind on occasion! The answers lie in thinking against the grain and tackling something new! How much worse can things get considering today's profit margins and stagnating sales, described by many experts as disastrous?

The "toothpaste expert" can be an important partner of the category manager (cf. the section on "It is not purchasing which is decisive, but the marketing concept") and play a successful role in his team. The dm over-the-counter discount drugstore chain, for example, does not have traditional purchasers any more, just assortment managers and teams.

The problem of managing a large number of products is illustrated again here by the example of bicycle accessories in a large hypermarket. The numbers are symptomatic for the inability to solve these problems. But they also show the large reserves that exist and the amount of waste involved in failing to get to grips with basic principles and details. In any case, it would be more worthwhile for any company's management to tackle this problem than to meet for lunch with a supplier who is also a friend or to attend a convention supposedly to learn about the latest scientific findings and practical applications.

The hypermarket in this example is a highly profitable outlet in a large, well-known food chain in Germany and is located in a small town in northern Germany in a rural setting. On 2,200 square meters of floor space, they earn annual sales amounting to 13 million euros. Low rent and good personnel productivity contribute to above average contributions by this store to the company's earnings. The non-food share of total sales volume corresponds to the average of other, comparable outlets in many companies who frequently offer comparable product ranges – including bicycle accessories.

In the bicycle accessories category, a total of 182 items are on sale. The shelves are filled by rack-jobbers, suppliers who visit markets direct, maintain inventory and reorder themselves. Retailers gladly accept a service like this because it reduces the need for costly personnel. What's more, the rack jobber is also an expert who can handle the job better. The mistakes and shortcomings that I would like to point out here, however, are not only related to the marked self-interest of the supplier and the lack of checks by the store. If the retailer's own employees did the work the situation would not be any different unless special methods were applied, such as those described above.

First – without examining the figures to start with – there are few notable points to be made regarding the assortment structure, and these observations can be made without getting involved in deep, quantitative analyses. The product range includes such things as chain guards, pedals for touring bikes, handlebars and two different saddle designs. Anyone with some bicycle experience knows that he has hardly ever changed his handlebars or had to replace the chain guard. But if he did, he generally would have gone directly to a cycle shop with a large enough selection to deal with a generally complex problem, and may well have had the replacement plus other assembly work done at the same time. The logical conclusion ought to be that products such as this do not belong on the shelves. More than one model of this relatively costly item would have to be stocked in any case. This conclusion can be reached without knowing the figures. This is exactly the suggestion which the Nobel prize winner Gerd Binnig makes when he explains the link between "ignorance" in the sense of getting along without information, and creativity.

Well, the figures confirm our assumption. The number of chain guards sold monthly on average over the course of a year is 0.3 units, for touring pedals the figure was 0.9 units. And it is even questionable whether these can be put down to genuine sales or were possibly the result of inventory shrinkage, which includes theft.

The core of this problem, however, stands out very clearly in the following numerical context which proves that there is something wrong with the management of such a business. One hundred and eighty-two items are in the product range, 56 of these selling fewer than 1 unit per month; these figures are more in line with a jeweler's selection than with a hypermarket which is customarily geared towards mass consumption needs with fast-turning stock. But nobody is familiar with these contextual issues. They pay too little attention to the details. They do not question the make-up of product range enough and why it is a good thing to employ rack jobbers.

New close-to-customer procedures are much more important than the painful exercises which take place at headquarters in an effort to get control over the reams of data. McKinsey director Peter Barrenstein may have recognized the profit margin disaster but he does not resolve it by demanding:

"Managing the data produced by integrated merchandise management systems must compel companies to set up new purchasing and sales analysis systems. You cannot just toss these data onto the desks of the department heads. The figures must be processed in a way which makes them useful in practice."

With the data from the electronic scanners you may have increasing control over the kind of imbalances revealed by the above bicycle example. However, it is always people who have to analyze the results. Here too, less is often more. And thinking without figures can still replace some complicated analyses. The "toothpaste philosophy" can also be applied to bicycle pedals and instant soups.

Less is more

All business systems, the organization, communication, even the scope and type of meetings are determined by the number of items in the product range. Metro, or even Karstadt, the higher-end department store, with over 100,000 items, have to take a different approach but even Tengelmann with its supermarkets and some 15,000 items has to do almost everything differently from ALDI. This cardinal difference has not been properly appreciated, even by specialists. Frequently the experts have been overly simplistic, pointing to the company's frugal store interiors to explain successes and differences. That automatically means that not everything at ALDI can be transferred to other companies. But what counts is the basic idea, for example, that for the customer each item is important and retailers must answer the question of how to deal effectively with this difficulty. This problem is covered by "tooth-paste philosophies," but also by the important insight that the suppliers should not make product-range decisions.

ALDI has never changed its iron principle regarding product range, even if it often looked like it to outside observers. But when 25 frozen food items were introduced, 25 other, weak items which were no longer basic household necessities were eliminated. The product ranges were changed and updated, restructured, but there was no increase in the number of items.

Nevertheless, competitors or trade journals repeatedly forecasted the end of the concept, foresaw it flagging: "now ALDI (finally, definitely, no doubt about it) will be compelled to widen its product range." In other words, now ALDI must become like all the others. Then it would be operating under the same conditions as others, and the competitive edge which had irritated competitors for so many years would be lost. Even for insiders such as myself, this is precisely one of the most admirable achievements of ALDI's business policy, of a strong culture, that it has not succumbed to the temptation of widening its product range. After all, surely another 50 items would not make such a difference? Surely they could mean a 5 percent increase in sales. Taking into account ALDI's size in Germany alone, that would translate into 2 billion euros. Would that not be extremely tempting to any other company – in view of the fact that most retailers are revenue-hungry?

ALDI's limited number of items enables it to benefit from consumers who, according to the opinion of trend researchers, like their products simpler, more durable, cheaper and plainer, and who are tired of being confronted with too many new products. The American futurologist Carol Farmer, speaking at the convention entitled Modern Market Methods (MMM) in Munich in 1994, referred to the 1990s as a "less decade" i.e. "less is more." But that also means lower costs and lower gross profits or profits margins on individual items. The enormous variety of products on offer today is quite a strain on customers, not only in terms of time. The trend researcher Matthias Horx says:[31]

"The consumer would like to be relieved of too many new products. He wants products on offer to be simpler, more durable, cheaper, plainer and ecologically sound."

Today, many customers are glad on occasion to do without the enormous selection, provided they can be sure that the product they quickly grab off the shelf is a good one. ALDI takes the strain off its customers. How difficult it is to pick out good salmon with any degree of confidence when there are several varieties on offer. I am quite happy to buy my wine at ALDI for 3.97 euros, knowing that it has been carefully selected and that I can rely on its quality. Hundreds of tasting sessions during my years at ALDI have, of course, given me greater confidence in its products than normal customers can have. But buying wine at another supermarket can be a major problem. Not only due to the fact that similar qualities can be priced between 6 and 8.50 euros.

Being spoilt for choice is another difficulty – and the quality even of higher priced wines need not necessarily be good. Today, ALDI even sells a French Margaux red wine (1993) at a price of 8.99 euros. Assuming traditional costing methods at ALDI's competitors, this wine would be at least in the 17.50 euros price bracket. This is another new item in the product range, following the successful introduction of champagne several years before. Champagne, priced between 8 and 10 euros, is now actually part of the standard product range.

Success is not decided by purchasing but by the marketing concept

When the cost price of inventory, i.e. the value of purchased goods, the purchase price, is considered as a cost factor, it is regularly the largest one in retailing. Sixty to 80 percent is very common. But it would be wrong for companies to conclude they have made a decisive contribution towards business success if they – as they may believe – secure good purchase prices.

ALDI's success is not ultimately based on purchasing – as many competitors believe – but on the selling-out side, on its sales and customer orientation strategies. Naturally, the company has to try to get the best conceivable terms in its negotiation. But of course not even ALDI knows exactly where it stands at the end of the round. It is by no means certain that ALDI always gets the best purchase prices in comparison with their competitors – and in view of the manufacturers' complicated and confusing terms and conditions, it would also be extremely difficult to prove.

In many companies there is too little thought given to core questions. More important than the question of purchase prices is something else:

"Why should customers shop in my store?
Why should the customer select my product?

This question, the core question for marketing and corporate strategy, applies in virtually all companies and institutions, from car makers to hotel chains to symphony orchestras. It is a simple question of strategic direction, of a company's concept. A vaguely worded statement like "we want to offer people good products at reasonable prices" is an inadequate response.

Unimaginative attempts are made to tempt customers with special offers. Purchasers and suppliers meet and work out their annual programs. Producers want to boost one item in particular, and retailers comply in exchange for a special payment (promotional discount or incentive discount).

ALDI, on the other hand, puts together its product range based on its own considerations and, primarily, taking into account its own customers' needs. Suppliers' terms and conditions do not play any role at all in the product range strategy, while at their supplier-oriented competitors they are often the only "strategy" they have. Thus, despite what is called the bargaining power of retailers, the retailers become the sales departments of the manufacturers. Those working in sales may not be satisfied with it, but nobody complains any more. It is as if this situation were unchangeable. Another advantage for ALDI.

Erwin Conradi was once very explicit about this subject:[32]

"I feel that the customers will favor those companies and distributors who adhere to a clear mission, establish a recognizable identity and demonstrate credible competence."

Who would want to deny that ALDI has fulfilled these demands? What about the others? Of course all drive hard bargains, undoubtedly including Metro. But what most experts mean by and designate as "purchasing power" is in fact "selling power": the ability to achieve high sales figures. Selling power is not part of or the result of purchasing power, although purchasing power in this context can provide support. The main factors of purchasing power lie elsewhere: sales concept, products, qualities, prices, locations, marketing.

Success is decided by the "clear mission" and not the advertising allowance from the supplier, which critical observers have referred to as the "wedding gift." If a supplier wants to place a new item on retail shelves, he must come up with something imaginative to get retailers' approval. Since retailers are always in need of money they demand that manufacturers pay a certain sum to get their item listed. Since retailers do quite a lot for the article – they present it on their shelves – money must be paid. These amounts are then put into the funds for outstanding achievements of the purchasers. How can purchasers prove how successful they were? Whether any specific purchase price can be called a success is anybody's guess. Perhaps too much was paid. But if the purchaser by the end of the year has "saved up" a nice pile of money, then it is a success. Such sums are even included in the annual budgets. But the advertising allowances reveal nothing about whether the purchase price is generally "appropriate." And of course the suppliers build such extras into their budgets in advance.

Retailers have developed many ideas in this context to compensate for their own lack of creativity on the conceptual side. Some examples are:

- *Anti-delisting discounts:* Manufacturers are required to pay contributions to assure that an item already in the product range will not be de-listed.
- *New listing kickbacks:* If they want a new item put on the shelves they must pay for it.

- *Anniversary premiums:* If a retailer celebrates an anniversary – whether the 10th or the 35th – a financial birthday present is expected; on its 90th anniversary Edeka sent out a call for contributions to the manufacturers which read like this: ". . . if you make available to us a one-time contribution of 25,000 euros, the sales fireworks can take place as scheduled this coming fall . . . ."[33]
- *Subsidies for opening a new distribution center:* A new distribution center costs the retailer plenty of money – this calls for sponsors.
- *Support for foreign expansion:* If the supplier wants good prospects of his own "overseas presence" being established by his items being sold beyond his own borders, then he had better make an investment; this may, in fact, already be "justified" by the fact that the supplier is "permitted to continue" his domestic business for the time being.
- *Extended shop opening hours discount:* when the German law regulating retail business hours extended the closing time from 6.30 p.m. to 8.00 p.m., the supplier was given the "enormous opportunity" of being permitted to have his goods "exhibited" on the retailer's shelves for an extra one and a half hours.
- *Sales interruption remuneration:* If non-delivery or late delivery (missing items in the shops) cause sales losses, compensation is claimed. But since the causal relationship is very difficult to prove and quantify, retailers go so far as to demand lump payments as compensation.
- *Junior discount:* This is retailing's latest creation. According to the 30 May 1997 edition of the German trade journal Lebensmittel-Zeitung, Tengelmann has issued an oral demand to manufacturers to grant a junior discount the "smooth transfer from on generation to the next," as the business changes hands from Erivan Haub to his son Karl Erivan.
- *Future bonus:* An invention of the "Nuremberg Federation." The long-standing suppliers of the cooperative for the purchase of household goods, recently barely saved from disaster by a composition, were asked to contribute to strategic restructuring by making a one-time bonus payment. Some of the same suppliers had already saved the company by dropping demands for unpaid debts.[34]

In comparison with the above some of the conventional discounts sound altogether harmless:

- Cash payment discount
- Quantity discount
- Merchandise category discount
- Item cash payment discount
- Delayed payment

- Promotional discount
- Delayed bonus
- Incentive bonus
- Performance remuneration
- Central remuneration
- Remuneration for lowest complaint rate
- Remuneration for product range growth
- Remuneration for selling space increase
- Media-related remuneration
- Entertainment terms
- Order set subsidy

Manufacturers feel compelled to give in to retailers, afraid that they might lose the business relationship. The reason is often that the products themselves are similar to the point of being interchangeable, and the utility value they have for the consumer is not very distinctive. In short, the question of why the retailer should have the product on his shelves cannot be clearly answered. Innovations are in short supply. But a few companies, such as Ferrero, tackle this task with gusto, high sales, good profits, and a strong position vis à vis the retailers. You have to look far to find another food company with brands as strong as Ferrero's (Kinder-Überraschungsei, Nutella, Mon Chéri, Rocher, Raffaelo).

The underlying reasons for such incredible discount policies cannot be found in a general weakness of an industry which in Germany shows sales amounting to 56 billion euros and employs over 500,000 people. The real reason, in my opinion, lies in strategic issues, in poor leadership and organization, and poor utilization of employee creativity. According to a study by Andersen Consulting[35] 40 percent of the employees at German companies have given up psychologically and have ceased applying themselves to thinking about the welfare of their companies.

ALDI does not pursue this sort of "discount policy." The purchase price is stated as net/net – after subtracting all the discounts which have no interest whatsoever for the purchaser. They concentrate on essentials, specifically, their customer needs, on their company's most immediate mission.

The consequences of such a retail policy are simple:
High advertising allowance + weak mission = modest success
Low advertising allowance + strong mission = major success

In an essay appearing in the *Lebensmittel-Zeitung* in 1994 entitled "Managing the challenge," Bernd Biehl wrote that the omnipotence of purchasing departments in Germany over recent decades has developed into the holy of holies of retail companies. The purchasers are evaluated by the theoretical gross margins, the differences between sales and purchase price, they have achieved.

Apparently at many companies the purchasing department even has the final word on sales prices. At ALDI, one of the most important business decisions, sales price, is made by the top management, i.e. the general managers and the administrative board.

A new strategy introduced by the German retailer Plus also seems dubious. It now wants to focus on the performance indicators "gross income" and "turnover ratio" – the customer is but dimly perceived, out there in the fog. "Gross income is the difference between the sales price and the purchase price. If one assumes that the purchase prices for each individual item are relatively fixed, Plus can increase its gross income only by means of two measures. It can increase sales prices. Success seems uncertain. But it can also make changes in its product range, because gross income is also the total from the sale of all items. Yet a successful outcome is questionable here as well if everything is seen only in terms of gross income, while the customers' needs only play a minor role.

Even more difficult to visualize is what is really meant by an improvement in "turnover ratio." Determining the quotient of turnover and inventory (the number of times the inventory kept in hand is sold on a monthly basis: sales of 10 million and inventory 2 million mean a turnover rate of 5 times per month) can hardly be called a major strategy. Inventory optimization to achieve effective logistics is of course a must, increasing sales is a good objective. The question is: How? Strategic considerations must focus on the customers – and nothing else.

One of the main consequences of the frequent lack of a holistic view of customer needs and the business concept is agressive promotional campaigns by the manufacturers in the form of eyecatching store displays that clash with the store's layout and upset organizational processes. Not to mention the usual surplus inventory which, after the campaign, ends up in the store's back rooms or is somehow squeezed onto the regular shelves. Such developments – which, after all, have continued for decades – result from mistaken ideas about the real success factors in retailing, and they, too, have also led repeatedly to mistaken "explanations" of ALDI's legendary success.

Today, in many places, new, close-to-the-customer organizational formats are being demanded and discussed. With the new-fangled concepts of "efficient consumer response" and "category management," people are trying to change the conventional ways of thinking. It is questionable whether the widely propagated concept of efficient consumer response can bring this about. Firstly, because once again, the new thinking is highly complex. But after all, simple methods cannot be sold so elegantly via a multiplicity of conferences and complex but profitable software.

Excursus: Efficient consumer response (ECR)

Efficient consumer response (ECR) is commonly understood to be the holistic coordination and control of the merchandise and information flow between manufacturers and retailers. The system components or subjects included in this are:

- Product range optimization
- Promotional sales
- New product introductions
- Manufacturers' selling-out concepts
- Holistic customer management
- Continuous goods supply
- Data carrier exchange

Using electronic data interchange (EDI), merchandise flows are supposed to controlled, optimized and documented. Data which are collected through modern scanners in the stores can help create the basis for optimization – for example, modern space management (floor space and shelf optimization in-store) and the design of an optimum product range balance. The goal is to realize saving potentials on both sides by the best possible delivery of goods and services to the customer and optimum inventory management. The "basic philosophy" of ECR is also said to be serving the common customer, the consumer, better, more quickly, and more cheaply.

It has been recognized that joint action has its advantages. But then the question of "fair" distribution of the savings arises. Consultants are said to have promised prospects of optimization potentials in the value chain amounting to between 7.3 percent and as much as 10.8 percent of sales. If you start at zero? Even if the manufacturers and the retailers divided this sum amicably, German retailers could at least triple their profits and have some left over to give the consumer.

The ECR Board Europe, a body consisting of producer and retailer representatives, has published "14 concepts" in an "official score card," a standardized checklist. Consultancies involved in the ECR believe that "the successful retailers of the future will implement the organizational changes related to ECR and reduce internal friction losses." Thus "the introduction of ECR requires marked experience in change and conflict management." These assessments – like so many other concepts – probably suffer from substantial exaggerations, of the kind the industry has been particularly familiar with since the discussion about "direct product profitability" (DPP) and which are being repeated in the case of category management. The implementation of ECR and its components is nothing other than daily work on details.

Over-inflated words and ideas for the most obvious subjects and tasks? What are we supposed to think of sentences such as "trade marketing is becoming the interface for business relations with retailers"? Or: "Brand-focused marketing plans are merged into one category plan"? Savings amounting to as much as 10.8 percent of sales? Confusion spread by over-blown language and slogans are hardly helpful to companies.

What is the real reason why this kind of process has been developed? Surely a legitimate question, in view of the obvious nature of ECR. I suspect that companies are short on other insights and convictions. Perhaps what they are lacking is a clear, strategic direction or a clear, goal-oriented leadership, maybe management lacks cultural elements. In any case, one insight is missing: retail means detail. But that applies to other industries and economic sectors as well as to many other aspects of life.

The realization of shorter waiting times simply goes without saying. The goal of standardized transport packages has been pursued for a long time, by harmonizing box and palette dimensions for other thing. Electronic data interchange has been around for many years. That they are attempting to standardize this was also to be expected. And there is nothing new about retailers and manufacturers basically having to agree on delivery frequency, inventory levels, delivery periods and planning and scheduling techniques for every single product. That has always been the case. And it was always a goal in retailing to use these means to limit inventory, but also, on the other hand, to reduce the joint logistics costs (delivery frequency and volume) since this makes it possible to reduce prices. Agreements and discussions between the partners, of course, also permit optimized production and inventory management on the manufacturer's side. The cooperation which is currently being so intensively discussed cannot be something completely new. All of these elements are commonplace!

Basically, ECR is thus nothing other than the application of the kaizen principle in the cooperation between manufacturers and retailers – except that ECR provides people with a nice, handy term. However, it does not involve the implementation of a genuinely new system, but the realization of many small improvements in sequence or in parallel, combined or independent of each other. One can only really advise at this point: do everything you can, step by step, grope forward toward solutions as ALDI and Einstein did. Avoid building any complicated new systems. Perhaps even the many conferences on this subject are not so much important as entertaining, welcome distractions in the midst of managerial stress. The 2nd ECR conference with its guest speaker Ignacio Lopez, who made the CIP[2] popular, as the kaizen system is called at VW, attracted 1,600 managers from industry and trade to Amsterdam in 1997, making it the biggest industry meeting ever held in Europe. One thousand six hundred business representatives who apparently also had the good will to improve relations between industry and trade. One positive point is surely the intention to reward genuine improvements financially as well. A "fair" system is certainly better than passing out anniversary or junior discounts. Only, it will not work. These discounts will presumably continue to exist over and above the others.

For example, the discount drugstore Schlecker announced to manufacturers that it had introduced ECR which meant an efficient logistics system. And that meant it now expected better terms and conditions. But there are also those like the Beiersdorf sales manager Jürgen Seefeld who say that ECR has nothing to do with terms and conditions. He is right, but judging by the negative reactions of his audience at the Amsterdam ECR conference, his opinion will not prevail. Could ECR in the end just mean: Endearingly Chic Reductions?

If people seriously want to work on easing relations between manufacturers and retailers it would be more helpful to apply themselves to developing a few ideas for the annual discussions and purchasing negotiations instead of frantically attempting to get into bed with new sciences.

On the other hand, cooperative ventures and discussions are always useful. Making trust the basis of negotiations and developing it between the partners using the Harvard concept – solving the other person's problems, revealing one's own intentions, not playing poker, but negotiating in such a way that the partners will look forward to the next meeting[36] – is sensible and necessary in order to achieve good results. In this sense, any efforts to apply ECR and category management can only be welcomed. In any case, a new hot issue will be useful in making industry focus on improvement opportunities.

Many of the claimed effects of the new ECR, however, are very questionable. The frequently cited, novel discounts that are linked directly to the sources of savings, such as the premium for ordering whole truck loads, or by the full pallet, are in fact nothing new.

The number of items traded remains much more efficient and effective in its impact on the revenue and costs of all those involved. Many fine points in the processes are addressed using ECR and can be improved, but the decisive point is the optimization of the product range – the ECR supporters call this "efficient assortments." In trying to optimization assortments together, however, the partners will find themselves banging their heads against a brick wall. The retailers are the decision-makers when it comes to attempts at optimization. The manufacturers' influence lies in their pricing strategies.

But optimization based only on all the scanner data imaginable will fail organizationally. The variety of options tends theoretically towards the infinite: product variants, alternative manufacturers and brands, different store concepts within a company – and on top of this different customer shopping habits at different locations at different times – are simply too much to handle. What is the answer? Rigorous decentralization and delegation. Principles and priorities together with the combination of Einstein's "I grope my way forward" and ALDI's no-nonsense simplicity are the only help. The use of scanner data can certainly be of great benefit to all parties, provided it is geared towards intelligent handling of the important data in the spirit of "less is more."

ALDI, for example, has been practising the "cross-docking" described in the ECR system for nearly 30 years. It was invented by practitioners in the ALDI distribution centers, developed and fine-tuned over the years following the kaizen principle with a passion for good detailed solutions. ALDI did not need to send representatives to a conference in Amsterdam for this – which would have cost 2,500 euros just for the travel expenses for two people.

Cross-docking in the ECR concept is a way of shortening the supply chain within the retailer's warehousing system. Products received by the distribution center are not held any longer than 24 hours. They are then delivered directly to the stores, without ever touching the distribution center's shelves. Ideally, the product is moved directly across the dock from the in-bound truck to the store-bound truck, i.e. it is cross-docked. ALDI has been practising this policy for a long time with fast-moving items such as beverages, sugar, eggs – so-called pallet goods. They called it the "open stack area." Optimization measures in shelving and planning have always been an important part of the philosophy of minimal costs. ALDI has always had an influence on easy-to-ship packaging which must be harmonized with the pallet size. ALDI just did not know that this approach was referred to as ECR and that consultancies could make a lot of money with it.

Excursus: Category management

Category management means professional assortment planning, which is often seen as an aspect of ECR. The ECR Europe Board has supplied a definition: "Category management is a process carried out jointly by retailers and manufacturers in which product categories are run as strategic units to improve profits by enhancing their value to the customer." This too was turned into a science.[37]

Category management basically involves organizing procurement and cooperating with suppliers and sales. The goals are to improve customer relations and increase the size of shopping baskets: in short, to increase turnover. The "category manager" at the retailer cooperates with his partner at the manufacturer, the "category captain." He is responsible for the "performance" (in plain English: the success and further development) of the category: for procurement, marketing, merchandising, logistics, sales and for the use of information technology. That is not actually an issue the manufacturers should have a hand in. Category management is an attempt on the part of retailers to control the difficult management of tens of thousands of items, assortments, new product introductions and sales promotions – but it is nothing new, and it is not the key to solving the problems involved either. The questions the category manager has to ask himself used to be asked by every purchaser, sales manager or general manager. And procurement has in general always been organized by categories. The only element missing was that the process was not implemented from the source of the item through to the point of sale.

Each purchaser is assigned a category which he is in charge of from procurement to sale, including pricing decisions. This is comparable to the role of the product manager at the manufacturer. Plus, a German food retailer, is now advertising for senior and junior category managers. Is this the way Tengelmann, its parent company, will solve its problems?

ALDI never went to all that much trouble over complex systems and concepts. This does not mean that they failed to recognize the interconnecting structures here. On the contrary, a substantial share of ECR and category management thinking is implemented in the ALDI way, some of it has been in place for decades.

The "toothpaste philosophy" is an approach similar to category management which, however, shifts the many tasks involved to the point of sale, into the stores. ALDI, like many other companies, works with purchasers who are oriented toward categories. The fundamental conflict between purchasing and sales is solved by having the ultimate decisions made by the general managers, who are above purchasing and sales in the hierarchy. The reason for this simple solution is, of course, firstly the small number of items carried. This means that each individual item has relatively more importance and that blanket decisions for whole categories are unnecessary.

But ALDI is, as I described in Part 1, an ascetic company which applies itself to facts and the necessary operations. The absence of staff departments has always saved ALDI from carrying nonsensical extra weight. Line managers have better things to do than to tinker around with theoretical concepts – which does not mean to say that they do not examine all the innovations and ideas in a wide range of meetings. But they restrict themselves to those which come from those who know and those who are doing the jobs.

Advertising means informing the customer

By limiting advertising cost to 0.3 percent of sales, ALDI once more demonstrates its rigorous frugality. That does mean some 50 million euros per annum spent on advertising in Germany, but competitors are spending two or three times this amount for the same sales volumes.

ALDI advertising has always been customer information: information about prices and qualities, about the difference between its package contents and those of competitors. In contrast to normal practice, ALDI never had a slogan. It was simply not necessary and, in fact, would have only flown in the face of its policy of rationality, of factual argument. ALDI did not imitate the kind of advertising associated with branded goods or cigarettes. And it never released a cloud of colorful balloons or whatever. ALDI was just as ascetic with its advertising as with everything else. The advertising for the highly popular detergent Tandil differed completely from the advertising for a product advertised as "the official detergent" of top German football club *FC Bayern München*. ALDI never even engaged an ad agency, they only needed an agency to manage the commissions for the newspapers. Advertising and flyers were hand made, so-to-speak, by ALDI's own employees and using the original ideas, with no laborious briefing of advertising agencies. One administrative board member used to be particularly involved in developing the messages and designs of advertisements and flyers.

ALDI's advertising messages have always reflected the core of the company's concept. Customers apparently understood this, while competitors thought that the messages were slogans intended no more seriously than their own. The ads always carried as many items as possible, including prices – formerly up to 200 on one flyer.

Here are a few typical examples of messages appearing in ALDI newspaper advertisements and flyers. They appeal to rational, informed consumers and stand out in sharp contrast to the usual advertising by competitors which focuses on specials and attractive images. Since this time, however, ALDI has changed its advertising presentation somewhat and shifted its emphasis towards calling potential customers' attention to its non-food specials. ALDI South has even started to use colors in its newspaper advertisements.

Advertising messages from ALDI flyers

- "Empty promises don't pay. They won't win customer loyalty. Customers are loyal because they are convinced. Every time they shop."
- "Value for money is a proven fact in our stores; our price lists contain up to 200 individual prices."
- "Our guarantee of quality makes every purchase a safe choice. The simple words 'I don't like it' suffice. We accept the return and pay back the price."
- "Try it . . . we back up our quality assurance by the many free samples in our ALDI stores . . . The free samples give you a chance to judge our items yourself – without any obligation to buy – which is why the item is not sold at the table containing them."

- "Compare . . . our price lists are designed so that they not only help you to make comparisons easy, they also enable you to check the quantities as well. The dot and the quantity in front of the item tells you that this item is also frequently available in other sizes. The differences are often imperceptible, or barely perceptible, to the eye. So it is better to look not only at the price, but also at the quantity.

The basic idea behind the advertising was that price lists containing 200 items encouraged consumer confidence, even if we could not expect customers to remember all of them.

One particular single exchange of blows, typical of ALDI advertising, occurred in 1977 with a newcomer to the discount business, the Leibbrand subsidiary Penny which today belongs to Rewe. On 16 September 1977, Penny advertised in newspapers and in their store-front windows with the slogan:

"Nobody is cheaper and better"

ALDI immediately responded using a tactic prohibited in Germany, comparative advertising. At the time this was a fight between Klaus Wiegandt, until 2000 the spokesman of the board of directors at Metro AG, on the one side, and Otto Hübner and myself on the ALDI side, supported by our enraged general manager Gerhard Bohnenstengel in Seevetal. We were highly upset, but we also felt it was a sporting challenge. ALDI's counter-advertisement looked like this:

"Nobody is cheaper and better"
    claims Penny-Markt GmbH 2105 Seevetal 2 in ads and on eye-catching posters across the front of their stores. Well, far be it from us not to appreciate the performance of a competitor; and yet . . . take a look for yourselves.

"Nobody is cheaper!
    Really? But it didn't take us long to find the list of 50 items below, all of which had higher prices than in ALDI stores: (50 items were listed showing comparative prices)
For example:

| 500g linseed rolls | ALDI – DM 0.89 | Penny – DM 1.68 |
| 1 liter of Amselfelder wine | ALDI – DM 3.48 | Penny – DM 4.13 |

"Nobody is better!

Here, too, the examples were listed in the same way. For example, items with bigger packs or spirits with a higher percentage of alcohol.

During a friendly telephone conversation, the then top manager at Leibbrand headquarters, Klaus Wiegandt, admitted that the approach had been inappropriate. This closed the matter. Penny never did anything like this again.

Truth and fairness were always fundamental rules for ALDI's advertising. It seems that consumers have rewarded the company for it. ALDI itself never conducted any surveys on the subject.

Dealing with suppliers: Consistent and fair

ALDI was just as correct in its relationships with suppliers – many of which have continued for decades – as it was in its treatment of customers. In contrast to a view often expressed in the trade, ALDI does not conclude any long-term agreements with suppliers as a matter of principle. Many believe that ALDI signs such agreements to bind suppliers in the long term and somehow make them keep their mouths shut. Wrong. The magazine *Stern* was also wrong when it once said that the "penny pinchers" put "thumbscrews" on their suppliers. For ALDI the only thing that counts is that suppliers continuously supply high qualities, and of course, the prices always have to be competitive.

If anything goes wrong, there are very simple sanctions. The supplier who previously supplied, say, 20 distribution centers of an ALDI Group, might perhaps lose five centers. Only in extreme cases – and these invariably involve quality issues – does he lose them all. This principle of distribution center allocation also enables ALDI to test out new suppliers and expand their ordering gradually.

Nor was there ever any intention of making any supplier completely or even substantially dependent on ALDI. Such ideas may appear an obvious way of exercising greater influence and pressure on suppliers' prices. But this would also make the customer, ALDI in this case, dependent. Dependent on fluctuations in quality, internal problems of all kinds in the supplier's business up to and including capacity breakdowns. Even a collapse caused by the supplier himself could easily be blamed by the public on the customer ALDI. Under these circumstances it was much more intelligent to use alternatives.

And for retailers it is always more interesting if the supply market is made up of a large number and variety of companies. Every company can only survive in the long term if its profit margins are big enough- so it simply does not make sense to drive a partner into insolvency or – one step short of that – to kill his appetite for business. This has been one of the most important issues on the agenda between manufacturers and retailers for many years. Here too, ALDI has had a positive impact on the economy, in addition to its inflation-braking effect.

A current example is the manner in which ALDI handled the problems with bread supplier Geschi and its owner Horst Schiesser. Schiesser, a vibrant personality who became famous for having purchased Neue Heimat (at that time an almost bankrupt, huge real estate company) from the labor unions for 0.50 euro and later wanted to add the Treuhandanstalt, which handled the privatization of East German companies, for the same price, was for decades a reliable ALDI supplier. But poor investments after Germany's re-unification had evidently way over-stretched his financial resources. His company's performance in supplying, in the final stages, 1,100 ALDI stores was suffering – as mentioned earlier. But ALDI was initially understanding and reacted cautiously in consideration of a company which till then had been working well. Schiesser was financially supported by generous terms of payment. In place of the previous credit terms and payment periods normally offered to retailers by suppliers, ALDI agreed to either pay on delivery or even to pay in advance. This gave Geschi a lot of extra time. But poor management evidently made further decline inevitable. The business relationship was finally terminated when Geschi started supplying ALDI stores so poorly – out of 11 kinds of bread, only 6 were delivered in many cases – that ALDI's business was also suffering.

The industry is quite well aware that ALDI is a fair and reliable partner. The occasionally scandalous practices known in the rest of the business were never part of ALDI's policies. Today, when a major German food retailer takes over a smaller company, everyone in the food industry trembles. The acquiring company immediately compares all the purchasing conditions of the acquired company with its own. That is normal and useful, to improve a company's own terms and conditions or to enter new negotiations with new, larger volumes. But then something else happens, something incredible: if the small company had a lower purchase price than the large, acquiring company, the large company demands a credit in the amount of the difference for the past two years. Sometime it even subtracts the amount immediately from its next bill. That is pure power politics, and has nothing to do with fair trade practices! Perhaps the small company had capabilities that contributed to smoother logistics, or simply negotiated better. However, the manufacturer may also have made the mistake of telling its large customer that it was getting the best terms and conditions. Dishonesty and lack of credibility can come expensive.

Long-term ALDI suppliers appreciate the fact that there is absolutely no re-negotiating with ALDI.

That was never expressed more explicitly than in the trade newsletter Extrakte published on 20 August 1976:

"With all manufacturers and banks checking their lines of credit, the story of how ALDI is judged should also be told for a change. People know how much ALDI turns over in its over 1200 stores, how unusual its costing is. But banks and manufacturers clearly judge ALDI positively. ALDI not only pays so punctually you can set your watch by it. The company is also a fair partner:

- A price – once it has been agreed to – is not open to "re-adjustments"
- No discounts are demanded afterwards
- No unjustified complaints are made
- Suppliers are not "sucked dry"

The ALDI companies are seen by everyone as partners who know that they need good, capable suppliers that have to be allowed to survive, i.e. to earn money. However, officially appointed ALDI suppliers must be ready to deliver at all times. If the goods sell rapidly, if they prove popular and ALDI needs additional supplies, the owners have no mercy. Everything I have written here I have heard and had confirmed over and over again."

But the practice in the trade between suppliers and retailers generally looks quite different, and Helmut Maucher, Nestlé, regrets that no book has been written about how to deal with suppliers, adding that Kant's categorical imperative should also be applied here: retailers should treat their suppliers as they wish to be treated themselves.

Many, initially small suppliers, have grown with ALDI to true greatness, thanks to ALDI-like consistent, low-price, quality-sensitive strategies.

A group of sales agents have helped considerably in this regard and some have even profited handsomely by it. Reputable names have been associated with ALDI for decades: Max Roob, Essen, Schulte und Tatenhorst, Mülheim or Klaus Mahnke, Duisburg. Like brokers, the agents were looking for new products, new manufacturers. They checked product qualities, manufacturer capacities and prices for ALDI. That permitted ALDI, moreover, to work with a mini purchasing department employing six central purchasers (ALDI North). The advantage of lower personnel costs in purchasing is absolutely irrelevant here, although theoretically important. Far more decisive here, too, is for small units to be able to work together in a much less complicated way and with less friction. The question whether ALDI paid higher purchasing prices than it needed to in the end because of its purchasing agents can never be answered with certainty.

In the trade journals a rumor was recently discussed which stated that ALDI wanted to cancel its business agreements with its purchasing agents to add their profit margins to its own revenues. It appeared as if ALDI wanted to drop the previous way of doing business after it had turned out that a few purchasers had taken advantage of perks. It may be right to punish individual trading firms, but the author feels compelled to warn against giving up a very successful principle. Anger and disappointment about long-standing agents may also have been decisive for such fundamental considerations.

The corruptibility of employees, especially in purchasing, is a problem which all companies have to face, including ALDI. The purchasers move enormous sums, and ALDI is certainly at the top of the industry: an ALDI central purchaser shows a turnover of between 1 and 2 billion euros annually with his product category – that means a manageable 50 to 100 items. Quite a few suppliers do believe that a small, private subsidy could oil the wheels a little.

It seems impossible to minimize potential corruption in advance, or actually to eliminate it altogether. A purchaser is paid a salary which corresponds to his position in the company and his expertise. It is impossible to raise that salary to levels which would rule out bribes on purely material grounds. ALDI has not taken any special preventative steps, and I myself cannot see any sensible approach to this because the purchaser requires the trust of his supervisor when he negotiates. Otherwise he would not be a convincing negotiating partner and his creativity would also suffer.

Improved and more successful negotiations

A number of ideas can be derived from ALDI's relationships with its suppliers for generally improved relations between retailers and manufacturers. The current negotiating practices can be loosened up and focused more on the facts. Putting on the pressure and playing poker are not the best approaches if people want to continue working together in the future. A good guideline for successful negotiating is offered by the Harvard concept mentioned above, whose most important principle is that negotiations have been successful when both partners would like to continue to do business with one another in the future.

The points I have listed below are from my experience the most important for successful negotiations with suppliers:

- Drop what is known as the annual conferences. The end of the year is an arbitrary and random date. Issues should be handled as they arise and negotiations should not have to start under the pressure of a deadline. Manufacturers and retailers could agree to individual periodic meetings for specific product categories.
- In fact, every "annual conference" is a strategic conference. The purchaser holds discussions autonomously, bearing sole responsibility for their outcome once management and purchasing have defined their strategic and tactical positions. He makes the final decision alone.
- Purchasers should not go into negotiations with target margins, but rather with conceptual ideas (e.g. replacement of suppliers, items or similar matters). A clear distinction must be made initially between concepts and conditions. The toothpaste philosophy explained above can help achieve this.
- Nearly every supplier's sales to you can be increased by 20 to 50 percent. The question is whether this is really wanted and how to go about it. At issue are concepts, alternatives and options.
- Turnover always has priority ahead of margins. It is common knowledge that costs and profit, in the end, can only be covered by margins. But the basis of any business with a customer is turnover. The main thought of the purchaser and supplier must focus on the interests of the customer, the consumer – anything else is short-sighted.
- Purchaser, supplier and terms and conditions may never be allowed to determine the product range.
- Terms and conditions must not lead to pressure on volumes and quantities. The principle has to be that the customer (who, after all, is in a self-service store) makes up his own mind. Volume-based sliding scales and discounts rarely make sense.

- No agreements should be reached which, at a later date, can only be adhered to by tying yourselves in knots and using tricks.
- Find logistics cooperation and rationalization models. The ECR can be a source of ideas.

So it is not the purchasing terms and conditions alone which determine ALDI's relations with its suppliers. A company that produces private labels needs the trust of its client. This is usually developed over years of business relations. In the beginning, however, there is of course always a sort of "coaching" by ALDI. This concerns good quality standards and their precise definition, package designs and sizes, as well as questions related to the supplier's capacity and his ability to assure hygienic and reliable production processes. Many new suppliers already know what to expect from ALDI. They ask colleagues and they prepare themselves for a completely different sort of business relationship than is otherwise customary in the trade. One really important point remains – and all ALDI suppliers will confirm this: renegotiations during which attempts are made to upgrade terms and conditions for deliveries which have already been made do not occur. ALDI is interested in the continued survival of its capable suppliers. These relationships are practically symbiotic. But to some competitors thoughts like these are foreign.

Only cost advantages generate price advantages

A decisive foundation for success is provided by cost management and cost structure. These factors basically decide to what extent the company's management and its employees are able and willing to work on details. Penny's chief executive Emil Heinz emphasized at the LZ conference entitled *Discount in Germany* 1996:

> *"Nothing is more important than the price. The price advantage only goes to whoever has the cost advantage."*

Some aspects of cost management and cost structure are demonstrated by the following examples from ALDI's business practice, for intelligent cost management is a vital precondition of the discount system. ALDI was never stiff-necked or short-sighted in the sense that it gave an "order" to reduce cost category X by a certain percentage. Cost reduction was never forced. The basic concepts of value analysis played more of a role. When value analyses are conducted certain business areas or cost categories are examined against the background of how important or necessary they are to the delivery of the end product. What is not needed can be eliminated. The yardstick for cost management must always be the strategy of the company. Caution must be urged against sawing through the "strategic branch" on which you are sitting. If, for example, customer advice is one of the company's important strategic approaches, then any personnel cuts in this area must be carefully handled. In recent years the department stores were constantly facing this predicament: cut high personnel costs to the detriment of customer advice? ALDI always finds itself in this dilemma when it wants to avoid long lines at the cash registers, because these lines are frequently only temporary.

The fastest cashiers in the world

The ALDI cash register system is in itself a phenomenon. Today, as in the past, there are probably no cashiers in the world faster than those at ALDI. Long lines may be one of all customers' most frequently aired complaints – including at ALDI – but the typical opinion of most ALDI customers is better reflected by the statement once quoted on the consumer feedback page of the *Lebensmittel-Zeitung*:[38] "These lines are really fast. They are long, but fast. They are super-fast. I don't know why this is so, but it is." Another customer referred to the "electronic brains" in the heads of ALDI cashiers.

Formerly, the cashiers knew all the prices by heart, today they know the three digit item number of every item. Generally, the customer cannot pack away her purchases as fast as the woman with the "electronic brains" can key in the prices. Within two weeks, a cashier learns practically all the item numbers. The explanation for this, at first glance, unbelievable performance is the enormous amount of repetition in keying in the individual items.

Nor is there another cash register system as reliable as ALDI's. Comparisons of price labels in the store with the amounts booked at the registers carried out during a survey of several supermarket chains showed excellent, error-free results only for ALDI. Those companies compared to ALDI, Allkauf, Plus, Massa, Globus and Penny, on the other hand, did not work without errors – another reason for the considerable trust which customers have in ALDI.[39]

Once the item numbers are in use, this system can do anything a scanner can. Of course this system is only suitable for companies whose product range is narrow enough. The ALDI register system features significant advantages in comparison to traditional scanners. The entry procedure is clearly faster, because the cashier need not cautiously and carefully read the scanner code into the system. She can key in the item even it is far down the conveyor belt. the system is much less expensive because no scanner is necessary, and it is less susceptible to break-downs. Here, too, the specific ALDI system of a limited number of items enables the typical simple solutions. When Germany changed from marks to euros ALDI South had to drop the old system (under which every cashier knew all the prices). They decided against the North system (every cashier knowing the three digit item code) and chose the scanner system. And here ALDI came up with a world novelty which no other major retailer, including Wal-Mart, had thought of before. ALDI required its suppliers to apply the barcode to the packages at three or four different places, enabling scanners to register the items faster.

ALDI was able to be this innovative because its decision-makers focus on business basics and not on synergies, mergers and diversifications.

But no system functions without efficient and capable employees. There is probably no other retailer with such skilled and friendly employees as ALDI. An experienced ALDI cashier also receives the highest wage in the industry, earning as much as 2,500 euros per month.

Shoplifting

In self-service retail outlets, shoplifting is costly. Comparable companies have shoplifting rates of up to 1 percent of sales. That would mean for ALDI an amount between 125 and 250 million euros in Germany alone. But ALDI manages to keep shoplifting down to a fraction of this rate. Work on details is the key to success here, too. In many ALDI stores observation walks are installed behind shelves from which employees have to systematically watch the customers to prevent shoplifting attempts. These observation walks are narrow, walkways behind the shelves, walled off by plywood, which are equipped with a small, one-way mirror observation window. There are one-way mirrors in the walls of the manager's offices as well.

Store interiors and product placement

It is often argued that "sales psychology" is the basis for ALDI's decisions regarding store fittings and merchandise placement. The interiors, it is thought, are kept so simple on purpose simply to create the illusion of being cost conscious. This is wrong. ALDI does not focus on impressions. Its focus is on costs and, in addition, making the customer an honest offer, without any "show." Customers are not supposed to believe ALDI is low-price. ALDI is low-price. The purpose is not to suggest this. It is a fact which customers experience when they themselves compare prices. Fitting out an ALDI store involves no other criterion than the use of purposeful, durable and low-cost materials. Shelves, aisle widths, and – if possible – even the length and width of the store itself are determined solely in terms of logistics (box size, pallet size, the maneuvering space needs for forklifts and similar matters).

In retailing it is common to place high-price items or items with larger margins at eye-level, or the narrow-margin items like sugar down low so that it is difficult for customers to pick them up or even to find them. At ALDI, on the other hand, merchandise is placed on shelves and pallets in the stores solely in response to logistical considerations. Appearance is not a factor. In the context of finely tuned ordering procedures, shelf space and position are determined above all by weekly needs, item characteristics and delivery frequency.

The ordering procedure itself is the simplest imaginable. As at Toyota and other Japanese manufacturers who use kanban systems it is based on: "replace whatever is gone."

Logistics

An interesting difference between ALDI North and ALDI South can be seen in their completely different approaches to store deliveries by truck. South operates without lifting platforms on the trucks, but has loading platforms at all its stores. North, on the other hand, only had platforms at stores where they could be easily attached. And therefore lifting platforms on all its trucks.

Today there is a trend towards situating stores on the edges of towns because sales and numbers of customers have continued to increase, and parking spaces are necessary for the larger average purchases. At North, too, this location policy has meant less and less need for lifting platforms on the trucks. This substantially reduces the cost of transport, but requires a mixed fleet which increases the complexity of distribution slightly because the vehicles must be appropriately assigned on a daily basis.

It can be maintained that the differences between these two basic systems cannot be quantified, because the feasibility of installing ramps at the stores remains a significant quantity which places restrictions on leasing locations. New stores outside the towns can be easily built to include loading platforms but in urban areas there are many stores whose positions rule this out. But, as is the case everywhere, there are always other options (Toyota philosophy).

In this instance, too, it is clear how useful a strict separation between ALDI North and South has been. They had no need to painstakingly work out a compromise, they could simply observe the other organization's experience with a different system. ALDI South is, as in many other cases, very much more rigorous in following principles and holding down costs, while at North they are somewhat more flexible.

Job sheets for maintenance workers

Tradesmen coming to carry out work in the stores, for example electrical repair companies, were compelled to keep a record of their hours worked on an ALDI form sheet. This form sheet is signed by the store manager and used later to check the invoice. It is a simple approach to dealing with a familiar problem which other companies have probably also discovered.

Personnel performance and productivity

There are still supermarkets around in which sales per month and per capita come to 10,000 euros. Good ALDI stores manage 100,000 euros. The reasons, of course, can partly be found in the different product range structures. This difference becomes interesting when you consider the annual wage increases. It always worked out in ALDI's favor if the wage increase was as high as possible, as was the case in their early years.

One example can demonstrate this effect. It is based on the assumption of an industry-wide, negotiated wage increase of 6 percent which for many years was a reality.

Prior to wage hike	ALDI	Competitor B
Total sales in millions	euro 20,000	euro 20,000
Wage total in millions	euro 600	euro 2,600
% of sales	3.00	13.00

After the wage hike

Wage total in millions	euro 636	euro 2,756
% of sales	3.18	13.78
Reduction in profits in millions	euro 36	euro 156
% of sales	0.18	0.78

Retail profit margins as a percentage of sales are generally 1 percent before tax. The competitor loses a substantial share (perhaps 50 percent) of his profit if this wage increase goes through.

But to retain the previous profits, and taking into account VAT, prices would have to be increased on average across the board as shown below:

at ALDI   +0.20%   at competitor B   +0.86%

In this way, ALDI's value-for-money lead kept on growing. Of course, companies increased their prices in a differentiated manner, for example larger increases for meat and cheese, where personnel service was required, and smaller increases for assortments in direct competition with ALDI.

The principle of ALDI stores

One ALDI flyer summarizes something that basically is not all that mysterious in any case. You only have to be capable of doing it, and do it. Karl Albrecht already talked about this back in 1953, and ALDI flyers have continued to propagate it for decades.

The principle of ALDI stores

Quality merchandise at low prices. This summarizes the goal and the recipe for success succinctly and accurately. And yet, how much planning, organization and detailed work are concealed behind this short statement. So perhaps it might be interesting to take a look backstage at a major operation whose self-assigned task is to offer top quality foods and other daily necessities at the lowest possible prices.

Worldwide purchasing

Long before an item is on the shelf in an ALDI store, everything is in place to obtain the best prices for enormous quantities. Negotiations are conducted which go beyond the usual limits of procurement negotiations. The goal is to realize a concept which is tailored to our large-scale purchases. Because our purchasers want more than to get a good price. Their goal is to conclude contracts in such a way that side-effects can be turned into purchase advantages. The ways and means of doing this are many:

A manufacturer with long-term, large orders might be encouraged to modernize his production facilities, to rationalize the manufacturing process.

Another supplier who sells most of his production to us might be convinced to stop advertising. Under the condition of a guarantee of purchase.

But also less significant agreements – such as the agreement that deliveries can always take place in full trailers – make for additional purchase advantages.

These examples should suffice. They demonstrate very clearly the targeted way in which the company works towards the lowest sales price as early as the purchasing stage; the wide ranging efforts made towards successfully, and effectively, rationalizing production. Worldwide – because the items in our product range come from many countries in all the continents of the world.

Low-cost transport

Every day enormous quantities of merchandise have to be transported to assure timely and reliable deliveries to ALDI stores. This massive movement of inventory works like clockwork. Dedicated employees, perfect organization, many years of experience and the latest transport equipment combine to ensure that the whole operation proceeds as economically as possible. Frequently, transport costs make up only fractions of a cent of the sales price of any individual item.

Tight assortment selection

For anyone who feels a strong need to select from among 20 different labels of, say, Scotch, ALDI will be a disappointment. The rule at ALDI is: "As few identical or similar items as possible." And the reasons for this are related to prices and costs. If we thought it was our job to provide a wide variety of any on item in a wide variety of sizes, then we and our customers would have to pay the price. By not having an enormous selection we are in a position to order enormous quantities of each individual item at the best possible price. Because even at the production level the most cost-efficient conditions have been created. But we not only get the best purchase price in this way, we also need less storage space. The item is turned around faster. That means that our stores and distribution centers can be smaller, and inventory does not cause a substantial interest burden. And for this reason, there is something else that you will not find in our stores: equivalent goods whose only differences are their labels being sold at different prices, though their purchase prices for the retailer are identical.

The business location impacts on prices

A significant share of the sales price is accounted for by the lease on the premises. Our efforts to bring down these expenditures as low as possible can be seen most concretely in the fact that we always do our best to select a store size which reflects expected demand. It is rare that a store turns out to be several sizes too large. We also do our best to avoid the high rents for the very best business locations. In other words, ALDI stores are usually not in the main shopping centers, but in side streets or on the edges of the shopping districts. Of course, having to go a long way is not always so pleasant for our customers – but it pays. Because low rents also contribute to low prices.

Sales without gimmicks

Rational selling – for us this is more than a mere slogan. When you enter an ALDI store you can see what it means. Sugar, flour, beverages, milk, laundry detergent and other items are presented for sale, untouched, on the same machine-loaded pallets as the manufacturer shipped them out on. All the other items are palleted once in the warehouse and moved to their position in the store. At that point it is usually just a matter of opening the box and the merchandise is ready for sale. None of our employees needs to unpack individual packages or put up decorations for the merchandise. We did not introduce refrigerated items, for example, until the refrigerators and the cardboard boxes matched our requirements. The refrigerators had to have enormous capacity and boxes had to be right size so that they could be placed neatly inside without any waste of space.

Conveniences such as home delivery are not provided by ALDI. And their absence also supports our low prices.

No frills

A look into an ALDI store shows that we do not spend one cent more on fixtures, fittings and façade than is absolutely necessary. Sober and to-the-point – that saves every ALDI store several thousand euros. And what that comes to is easy to imagine when you consider the large number of ALDI stores. We really do save gigantic sums – and these savings are reflected, again, in the prices. Not just once. After all, the fittings of an ALDI store do not last forever.

Where we do not turn over every cent

When quality is involved! Of course we do not neglect any opportunity which might genuinely improve our value for money. Only in one case do we make no compromises, and that is if reducing the purchase price means a loss in quality. Low prices at the expense of quality is not our idea of performance. And to ensure that people do not start thinking that these are just fine-sounding words, unlikely to be true, we support our claim to quality with the best possible guarantee imaginable: if the customer does not like the goods, he can return them. He only has to say: "I am not satisfied with this." The purchase price is returned without debate.

Information about long-term prices

At the end of all our efforts to sell as rationally and efficiently as possible, the final outcome is the price. The price of each individual item. Because we do not aim to prove our claim to being especially inexpensive just with a handful of specials. Each individual price is closely calculated and stands up to examination. Every price is a long-term price. The prices of our items only change in response to changes in the purchase prices.

These are not empty promises. We prove it over and over again.

Our price information announcements are designed so that they not only make price comparisons possible, but they also make it easier for consumers to take quantities into account. By adding a dot and the quantity in front of the item, e.g. 1 liter Amselfelder (a popular red wine), we indicate that this item is often offered in other sizes as well. These quantity differences are sometimes difficult or even impossible to detect by eye. So it is better to judge these items not by the prices alone, but by checking the quantities as well.

Our information also contains additional tips about such things as product sampling days in our stores, which permit customers to test the quality of our items themselves – guaranteed without any pressure to buy.

Open-minded customers

The principle of the ALDI stores, of course, could only be implemented because customers quickly recognized the advantages they were offered. They welcomed this sales system, although it demanded quite a bit extra from them (their shopping became somewhat more difficult).

Shopping at ALDI does not take place under such pleasant conditions as elsewhere. Longer distances – ALDI stores are not on every corner; occasional waits at the checkout counters; no extra customer services – just to name a few points – do not always make shopping at ALDI a pure pleasure or a "shopping experience to remember." But it is impossible to achieve both with one sales system: shopping as pleasant as possible, and prices as low as possible.

So we have rigorously put our money on quality and especially good value for money. Our customers' shopping experience should consist of getting good merchandise at low prices. And experience has shown that our customers prefer this sort of shopping experience because they do not have to pay for it – in the form of higher prices. On the contrary, they have more money because of the low prices.

ALDI, basically, has never changed its business principles. They have simply been updated, and adapted in line with developments. What has remained unchanged are the price and quality strategy, the number of products to a large extent, and the idea of the no-problem merchandise. What has changed – but in harmony with the concept – has been the locations. The need for more parking space meant that stores have generally been moved out to the edge of town and to more open spaces; refrigerated articles such as dairy products and frozen foods have been added and the non-food range has been substantially widened.

What is special about ALDI business principles?

Concept, idea, vision
Everything starts here. This rules a company and shapes it down to the last detail. A clear strategy and clear goals are the basis of any convincing business policy.

Assortment structure
A decisive retail function has always been the assortment function, i.e. the composition of items or offering of inclusive services to the customer, oriented towards the presumed expectations of the potential customers. The entrepreneur initially takes his decisions as a representative of his customers. He pre-selects. In doing this he has assumed the function of composing the product range. The customers can trust his selection, his qualities and his choice between various alternative options such as Maggi or Knorr in instant soups. Making this decision, this selection, requires courage. Not presenting the same product several times just because there are different names or brands available. ALDI follows the principle of keeping the number of items down to an absolute minimum, and offering as many different kinds as possible. The assortment structure, the selection of items, is carried out independent of suppliers' terms and conditions and prices.

Price strategy and costs
Low prices are always advantageous for customers independent of market conditions and what the competition is doing. Low prices are the point. The lowest possible costs are an essential prerequisite for these prices.

Advertising
Informative and trust-building

Business partners
Treat them as you want to be treated yourself: live and let live.

ALDI today
and a glimpse of the future

From discounter to cult object

Günter Ogger, who critically examines the retail business in his book *King Pin Customer: Set up and knocked down*, accuses ALDI and others of dubious purchasing methods and complains that consumers are offered a negative selection of retail goods due to the choice of the cheapest suppliers, in a process akin to selecting the chaff from the wheat. Commercially, Ogger considers the German retailers successful in Europe, but Germany's discounters are spreading into neighboring countries "like the plague."

It is difficult to view companies such as ALDI as "disreputable" simply because they are commercially successful. Besides, the wicked discounter compels its customers to give up everything which makes shopping pleasant. But apparently customers like to shop at ALDI. After all, they are free to shop elsewhere if they don't like it. The complaint is also raised that the goods are "lovelessly" piled on the shelves. But in what stores are they stacked with love? Could it be that there are other, more appropriate places to look for love?

The facts on the ground, reflected in customer statements, speak a completely different language – as a customer in the LZ consumer forum put it: "ALDI has something nearly puritanical about it, somehow more honest than these highly decorated supermarkets." The image of the company is repeatedly described in the same terms: "simple," "honest," "inexpensive."

An article which appeared some time ago in the magazine of the national German weekly newspaper *Zeit* (19 June 1997), written by Claudia Kempf and entitled "The ALDIans" shows that the ALDI stores have now become more than simply a "must" for all comers, they are the center of a cult.

The ALDIans

What has happened to ALDI? Shopping there is suddenly no longer embarrassing. It is a must. It used to be that only people on welfare and students shopped at the discounter owned by the brothers Theodor and Karl Albrecht. Today, an increasing number of the well-heeled are populating ALDI's no-frills aisles and filling their shopping trolleys and the tills of its nearly 3,000 stores. Have they just lost their brand name fever, or is this evidence of a new wave of German modesty? A new type of person is making a statement: Yes, I shop at ALDI.

Ute Noll, editor at Bild

Going to ALDI is fun when it is not so crowded – like on Monday morning. I mainly buy cleaning liquids there. But I also keep an eye out for the specials. I think it's fabulous that ALDI recently carried oleander plants. We bought three of them right off. That was just brilliant, we had been going to buy them anyway, and there they were. They were wonderful for the balcony. Shopping at ALDI is also fun because you can see so much and watch so many people there. It is almost like being at the movies.

Bettina Uhlemann, certified watchmaker

We shop at ALDI because you can find a lot of inexpensive items that do not necessarily have to bear a brand name, such as kids' clothing and diapers. The products are good quality. There are pajamas that I have already put through the washing machine and the tumble-dryer at least thirty times. And they are still in good condition. My husband thinks it's really "in" to shop at ALDI and sometime tries to get off early to go shopping there for me. I think he gets a kick out of these packages. He is always buying things like enormous boxes of cornflakes or extra-large cans of meat. For me it's completely unexciting, but he thinks it's absolutely great.

Helga Schmidt-Weilbrock, former hotel owner

Friends of mine told me about ALDI. We were drinking a marvelous champagne and it was from ALDI. Since then I buy my alcoholic beverages here and everything I need for parties or for the kids. After all, I can stock up my freezer wonderfully on their very good frozen foods. And on Thursday I always go to ALDI because that's when the fresh flowers are delivered. I like the spaciousness, the cleanliness, the good air and that the merchandise is always fresh. Having the items printed out on the receipts alongside the prices is also very practical. When you get home this gives you a complete overview of how much you have spent on what.

Dr. Götz Hartmann, manager

I buy at ALDI particularly because they offer value for money. The only problem with the specials is that they are difficult to get because of course many shoppers know that they are so good. That means that where there are specials there is a run on the nearby ALDI stores, for example to grab shirts with the right collar size off the shelf. Basically you can say that ALDI offers good quality – in the case of shirts, very good quality even – and that prices are lower than anywhere else. The great thing about ALDI is that we save so much that my wife was recently able to buy a convertible.

Heinz Rohn, graduate engineer

Since I retired I meet many of my acquaintances when I am out shopping. Especially here in the country, ALDI performs a social function, a place where people can keep in contact with each other while shopping. I buy staple goods here. What convinces me about the merchandise is its good price-performance ratio. But the specials are also attractive. Once I bought a camel hair blanket which was so nice that my wife wanted one just like it. At most retailers I would have to pay twice the price for the blanket. I also got a good price on an instrument for measuring blood pressure. But you need some luck with the specials. In one or two weeks, at most, they are sold out.

Stefan Zwink, architect

Actually, I only go to ALDI when I have decided in advance to go there, not by chance. They have a very good floor-care product that I like to use on my parquet floor. And of course we have a cooking club with three others, every-one takes turns cooking, and for such occasions a bottle of ALDI olive oil is a good thing. If the food items are really good we pick them up at ALDI too. It is well known that their champagne is very good. I know people who have bought out a store's whole stock of it. Not for a party or anything, just to stock up at home. I have not yet bought any specials at ALDI. I believe ALDI bicycles are worth buying. At their prices you could buy yourself a new one every year.

Gregor Schürmann, college lecturer and management consultant

Everyone tries to use their money wisely. Luxury can make sense if you can genuinely enjoy it, but I do not need brand name toilet paper. When it comes to laundry detergent I pay attention to quality. At ALDI you find the award-winning products, not anywhere else. Crackers, for example, things people have been buying since their college days, you may change the store where you buy them but you don't switch products. Primarily I buy household items, cleaners and everything I need for the bathroom. But there are also canned goods or jars that are brand-quality products although you cannot see it from the packaging. I always buy certain specific products, I would never buy any others there. But I always wonder how I manage to fill up a whole shopping trolley without having to pay more than fifty euros. That's pretty astounding, really.

Andrea Göke, senior manager

I enjoy shopping at ALDI and I frequently do because you get good quality at very acceptable prices. I buy nearly everything here with the exception of occasional fruit and vegetables or fresh meat. I also like the atmosphere. You can see where things are, and the whole selection of products is well arranged. I think its especially great that you can sometimes find products at ALDI which you never would expect. For example, last winter I bought angora underwear which is great for skiing. I was really lucky to have got it. Once I went to great lengths to find a practical hand vacuum cleaner which a friend of mine had. My local ALDI store did not have it. So I called up all my acquaintances who are also ALDI fans, and asked them to look for this vacuum cleaner. But unfortunately it did not work out.

Uwe Beyer, art director

I think everything here is great. When I shop at a supermarket other than ALDI I always burst into tears at the cash register because I know for sure I could have bought the whole load at ALDI for half the price. The things I mostly eat are the Brie and the salmon with its unbeatable sauce. Whenever I go shopping elsewhere I am paralyzed by the choice. At ALDI, on the other hand, for example in the case of coffee or cheese, there are only a few alternatives. And then there are the very intensive quality controls, and everything is always fresh because the shoppers buy like there's no tomorrow. Recently I bought myself a nice new hair dryer there, it cost seven euros and fifty cents, and it is so powerful it nearly blows your head off. It even fell in the toilet once, and it still works. Then I bought a tent at ALDI, a stereo, and I even used to have a television from there. But the greatest thing about ALDI are the girls at the cash registers. They are the fastest in the world. They rarely ever make mistakes and they always have a friendly word or two for every customer. For me the great challenge is to pack things away faster than the cashier can key them in and pass them on. I have never succeeded, although what I do is more like throwing things into the bags than placing them. At ALDI people of all ages and all cultural backgrounds come together. You see some of the most eccentric people. Once I met two construction workers who had picked up five trays of Hansapils beer. While they were waiting at the register they had already drunk five cans because they were emptying them at one go.

A flyer published by the Deutscher Gewerkschaftsbund (German Labor Federation) (see opposite page) shows how positive the public's relationship with ALDI is, sometimes almost a family relationship:

Frequently customer attitudes towards ALDI reflected gratitude, exhibiting the sort of genuinely personal feelings which no other company in the food industry has been able to evoke and which are most reminiscent of the sort of intimacy customers once felt at the "Mom and Pop" store.

Young people even hold "ALDI Parties" which simply have the theme of the "ALDI" label. Every guest must bring something bought at ALDI for the refreshments and wear something which is somehow related to ALDI. You can even buy T-shirts now with an ALDI-like logo, and besides the ALDI cookbook for adults, ALDIdente, a cookbook for kids has also been published, entitled ALDI Piccoli, written by Paula B. Spielhof and Karin Augenthaler. This book was created in cooperation with a club which calls itself the "First German ALDI Fan Club." The fan club, it says, "acknowledges itself as a supporter of the discounter ALDI and, by so doing, is working for a better, more honest, and more enjoyable future." But the ALDI Group has nothing to do with this. It knows nothing about it, and does not hear much about it.

Activities abroad

In 1976, at the AIDA congress in Geneva on the subject of ALDI, an Italian asked whether the ALDI formula also could be implemented in Italy. Only today, more than 20 years later, is ALDI on the way to answering this question. The Italians could therefore have marketed this sort of approach much sooner. But they waited until the first German discounters arrived. An American asked in Geneva whether ALDI's management and business principles were appropriate for use in countries around the world. If the principles of decentralization are mastered – witness McDonald's – then this problem is minor. I estimate that ALDI's foreign sales in 2003 amounted to some 15 billion euros.

Flyer issued by the "Consumer" work group of the German Labor Federation September 15, 1973

Do you want to throw your money out the window?

You need not pay exorbitant prices if you use your options!

Get value for money! Compare!
You determine the prices with your own money!
Every year you are losing a large share of your income to inflation!

There is no need for it!

Here are price comparisons you can use.

We went shopping for you:

Two shopping baskets with the same contents

with the same brand names or equivalent qualities!!!

The cost of one basket:	**DM 49.53**
The cost of the other basket:	**DM 28.40**

Come to our information stand and see for yourself.
Today, September 15, 1973 – 9.00am to 1.00pm Schillerplatz

Work group "Consumer Affairs"
at the German Labor Federation
District of Iserlohn

Author's note: Two baskets of merchandise, each consisting of 32 items, were purchased. The cheap basket at ALDI, the more expensive basket at another well-known German chain store.

Europe

The market shares of the discount segment in Europe in 2000 probably amounted to between 20 and 25 percent. In 1991 the discount share was estimated only as 10 percent of sales. If one takes the relevant items (same categories of products sold in the discount store and in traditional supermarkets) the market share of an ALDI in Germany would amount to some 40 percent.

Many experiments by food retailers in countries outside their own have failed. The Belgian attempts in The Netherlands were abandoned, the Dutch failed in Belgium, the Swiss and the French have failed so far in Germany. In fact, till now only one system of food retailing has been able to spread in Europe and even to the United States: the discount system. But ALDI's competitors have also expanded here, especially Lidl which in 2003 had some 3,300 stores in Europe outside of Germany.

ALDI has roughly 3,100 stores located outside Germany (in 2003), some 2,300 of them in Europe, and 740 in the United States and 60 in Australia. But there is evidence that the original attempts at "soft discounts" were less successful. Only the "hard discount" à la ALDI was really able to dominate the market. So the original "soft discounters" have turned into "hard discounters," or into neighborhood stores with widening product ranges.

Austria (ALDI South)

The first foreign venture of the Albrecht Group was the takeover of a small Austrian chain operation called Hofer in 1967. This name has been kept until today. At times, Hofer/ALDI has had enormous tremendous difficulties with the public authorities; the Group in Denmark had a similar problem. In 1975 the Austrians attempted to pass an "Anti-Hofer-Law." All food discounters were to be forced to sell milk, dairy products and bread, to insure that the population would be better supplied on a local level.

The reality in all countries, including Germany, always proved that such attempts at regulation never really had anything to do with supplying the population, but with concrete economic interests in protecting certain industries or interest groups. Among the leading opponents of Hofer and supporters of the "Anti-Hofer-Law," ahead of all the rest, was the Austrian retailer Konsum. Perhaps it would have been better if Konsum had redesigned its own corporate strategy: It no longer exists. ALDI/Hofer must have some 300 stores in Austria and sales amounting to 2 billion euros.

USA (ALDI South)

Karl Albrecht invested in the United States. In 1976 he took over the Benner Tea Co. in Illinois and now operates some 740 boxstores, as the Americans call these locations. Sales can now be estimated at $4.5 billion.

England (ALDI South)

ALDI South went into operation in the United Kingdom in 1990. This market, which is highly interesting because of its extremely high margins, probably went to ALDI South following a "tacit" agreement to leave the former GDR to North. However, the North, with its connections in the Netherlands, would certainly have had an easier time of it.

However, South is successful. From 1991 to 1994 sales – naturally due to expansion – rose sixfold. In 1998 there were just under 230 ALDI stores in the United Kingdom with sales of 1 billion euros. In 2003, it was estimated at 330 stores with sales of 1.9 billion euros.

The Netherlands (ALDI North)

North started its foreign activities by taking over a small chain operation owned by Combi N.V. in Zeist in 1975. The Netherlands later became an important staging area for entry into Belgium (initially Flanders) and on through Wallonia into France. This was an ideal development in terms of the important factor of language. Today, some 400 locations have sales amounting to 2 billion euros.

Belgium (ALDI North)

In 1976, when ALDI appeared on the Belgian market after acquiring the small chain operation Lansa N.V., the experts here, too, began to make their analyses and write their commentaries. In any case, the trade journal Trends published a very clever description of the new situation in 1978. A few quotes will suffice to give a picture of how the Belgians perceived ALDI's activities after ALDI had already been operating for about three years in neighboring Holland, with 80 stores: "ALDI is a unique phenomenon," is its conclusion. And further: "The brothers Albrecht, two self-made men, started in Germany with principles which had the established and major retailers shaking their heads. Leave the boys to it, they won't get anywhere anyhow." The journal correctly concluded: "The only standards are: quality and price" and "The whole system is based on the lowest possible costs which permit a low sales price and nevertheless a considerable profit." And, on the subject of competitors' reactions, the journalists wrote:

"The retail experts know that such a project was crazy for good reasons. The consumer wants a complete range of products at one location. A supermarket has a selection of about 5,000 items. The larger the selection the more customers you can attract. The consumer wants a pleasant shopping environment and luxurious store fittings. The majority of consumers do not buy totally unknown brands. ALDI sells too cheap. It cannot keep it up. Yes, and what else did we use to hear? In this country, the customer wants to be served. In Belgium self-service has not got a chance. Supermarkets: fine for America, it won't work here."

Well, the Belgian editor had done his homework and presumably read his "Karl Albrecht vintage 1953." By the way, ALDI did not get off to a better and faster start anywhere abroad than in Belgium. And as was often the case in other countries, ALDI was the first successful foreigner in Belgium. With 370 stores, ALDI posts sales amounting to roughly 2.1 billion euros.

Denmark (ALDI North)

In Denmark, where ALDI was never really able to establish itself, for many known, but also to date unknown reasons, the newcomer was met with a stiff resistance bordering on hatred.

Erik Sunström, chairman of the Association of Danish Grocery Retailers and Spar-Retailers, wrote: "I do not understand what 'they' want. The Danish retailers do their utmost and have to face tough competition among themselves."

In Denmark, protectionist practices also made life difficult for ALDI. It was forbidden to transport or sell long-life milk unrefrigerated. This was ultimately investigated by the European Commission and the European Court where the Danish government finally had to back down. In 2003 ALDI was operating some 210 stores. This does actually correspond to the market density relative to the population of Germany. Sales can be estimated to have reached some 800 million euros.

France (ALDI North)

Discount in France, a cultural revolution fifteen years ago, is now a hit: there are more than 1,700 stores, and 200 more are added every year. But these figures are probably substantially underestimated, as was the case in Germany as well in the early days.

In France, the land of the gourmets, ALDI achieved overwhelming successes right from the very start. Logistically and in terms of management, the launch was made very easy by the fact that it came from neighboring, French-speaking southern Belgium. In 1996 ALDI took over 74 Dia stores from Promodès. In 2003 ALDI was operating some 600 stores with sales tallying 2.5 billion euros, but Lidl already had over 1,000 stores. The German discounters divided up the French market, is how experts described the situation. The French see relatively few opportunities for themselves because the expansion, they believe, requires a large amount of capital – an assessment which is incorrect. The capital requirement is low in comparison with other retail investments. The difficulties, in my opinion, are generally related to implementing a simple concept with managers who have not learnt to act consistently and simply.

USA (ALDI North)

In 1978 I bought Theo Albrecht a small chain operation in the United States selling delicatessen, European wines and cheese specialties: Trader Joe's. A company in whose Hollywood store the most famous actors – but others as well – shopped in person, and to which the customer would drive nearly 100 miles. The founder was Joe Coulombe, one of the most knowledgeable and imaginative entrepreneurs I have ever met. He had laid the cornerstone for later success over many years with his customer-oriented passion, and not least with his famous radio ads on the classical music station KFAC under the title: "This is Joe Coulombe with today's words on food and wine." At the start of the negotiations the purchase was balanced on a knife's edge. Joe Coulombe was afraid for his company and his employees, as like the ALDI operation as fire was to water. Finally, Theo Albrecht's acquisition relied heavily on my close personal and confidential relationship with Joe Coulombe and his wife.

From this small initial investment an enormous asset has grown. Today Trader Joe's has acheived cult status and is well known all over the United States – selling delicatessen directly from pallets.

After the Essen ALDI Group's own discount activities were initially planned then stopped – I was already holding job interviews in Texas with candidates for the post of CEO – I went looking for an additional interesting investment for Theo Albrecht in the American food retailing industry. Albertson's in Boise, Idaho appeared attractive to me. Thanks to good relations with the majority shareholder, Joe Albertson, and the top management, the new major shareholder, the Theo Albrecht Foundation, was "welcomed" in 1982. With a solid 10 percent share this investment in an excellent company, which is ranked second in terms of sales in the United States after its merger with American Stores, was a good investment decision.

And now Australia and other countries

Nobody expected it: in 2001, Aldi South entered Australia and is earning overwhelming profits on its first 60 stores. Aldi North has entered the Spanish market with some 60 stores as well. And in Italy, Aldi is "ante portas." Other German discounters are already doing business there. Italy is said to be the most discount-crazy: more than 100 new stores open every month.

What will happen next? The big steamship ALDI is under way. The European Union is facilitating the rapid exchange of information, borders are open, and it seems entirely logical that there will soon be an ALDI organization in every European country. The euro, moreover, will lead to consumers being able to compare cross-European prices easily in the near future.

The multiplication of management for the local organizations will become increasingly simple with increasing size. Whether the administrative board in Essen will be able to manage the whole empire is an open question. As far as Mülheim is concerned, it is conceivable that they will be inclined to exercise control and will focus on fewer, very attractive countries – as in the day-to-day business. Aldi South, in addition, took a more Aldi-like simple solution for their foreign investment: they operate only in German-speaking (Austria) and English-speaking (US, UK, Ireland, Australia) countries – a way to master complexity.

The outlook

Rewe boss Hans Reischl forecasted not long ago that the discount system had passed its zenith because the full-liners had now got their costs so well under control that they could put a stop to its development. I do not share his opinion.[40] The false conclusion, in my opinion, is due to the fact that while the others may have improved – which is quite open to doubt – the system which the genuine discounters are operating is different.

The ALDI concept, the ALDI culture, the special organizational principles and the principles in business strategy form a relatively strict, holistic system. ALDI is a system, and the following applies:

The system is more important than the team.

Such influential systems can in principle be transferred to other companies and even to other industries and tasks, including cultural and political fields.

ALDI won its enormous competitive lead with its principle of simplicity, with its rigorous approach, and its work on details. ALDI was able to make use of the time in which competitors kitted themselves out with rigid organizational structures, looked down arrogantly on the newcomer, and maintained and expanded their complexity. But today, some have woken up and are in the process of dropping their old excess weight. But the markets will not really shake themselves up until the insight spreads that product range and price are the issues of retailing because that is what the customer is interested in.

One can only repeat "back to the basics, or "keep it simple"! An independent corporate culture with good organizational and business principles, focused on the core question "Why should the customer shop in my store?" will deliver solutions and positive developments. This is the only way German companies can meet Wal-Mart head-on. Wal-Mart should be taken very seriously as a new competitor. Not because Wal-Mart is twice as big as Metro, but because the principles of Wal-Mart and those of ALDI are so similar.

Computers are elbowing out canned beans

The share of non-food, or rather the share of ALDI "spot items" as they are officially known within the company, probably now amounts to over

20 percent of sales, which means some 5 billion euros. Originally this figure was merely about 2 percent when ALDI used to have a very strict rule: three spot items which had to be sold within three weeks.

Today, ALDI goes much further, though this undoubtedly causes problems. According to the present system, 20 to 40 new items are added every week, which can frequently mean up to 50 items in the non-food assortment at the same time. Shelf warmers or – properly speaking – remainders cannot always be avoided. When prices are lowered later to sell these remainders, credibility can suffer. Problems are also created if a store only receives eight of a highly popular item (bread-makers in the Hamburg outlets), because the purchasing or supply process has not worked properly.

Nevertheless, the Frankfurter Allgemeine Zeitung ran a commentary on the first sale in 1997 of the ALDI PC Medion/Lifetec, a high-spec 586 Pentium at euro 999, which stated:

"Who had expected this from ALDI? Something which can be sold by the thousands will sooner or later appear at ALDI. And that is where we picked this up, in a box for 999 euros off a standard Europallet: a minitower built around a 100 megahertz Cyrix 5x86, a compact computer modeled along the lines of other computers in the lower Pentium class. The name is Medion."

Experts estimate that ALDI has already achieved a market share of some 10 percent with computers after selling them for about 7 years and is considered to be the second-best seller of PCs in the German market. A total of 150,000 readers of *Computer-Bild* (the largest European computer magazine) named the ALDI computer the "most popular electronic release for the year 1998." ALDI received the "Golden Computer" for it. The magazine rated the Medion Professional as "very good."

Originally, the Golden Specials from Kaufhof delivered the model and the idea. Sales of consumer durables by food retailers are now traditional and highly significant. ALDI in this context is already considered one of Germany's leading clothing outlets. Tchibo now sells more non-food than it does coffee.

Here too, the narrow range of products, bought and sold in enormous quantities at extremely low prices without service, is the reason for the success. The basis is always the several thousand points-of-sale which only food retailers have at their disposal. But ALDI and Tchibo continue to carry their core assortments as always, unaffected by the new promotions.

Will ALDI keep its rigorous approach?

The expansion in non-foods is somehow bringing a fundamental change at ALDI. This is in addition to the widening of the product range: ALDI North expanded its range in the past years by 100 items with some more variations through "mixed" boxes which meant different kinds of the same item with the same price, quality, and size. For example, three different juices such as orange, grapefruit, and apple in one box.

There is in my eyes a serious shift in principles and a tendency toward a change in the system.

ALDI South – which carried 450 items for decades – today carries 650. The Mülheim side of the business was always considered the "orthodox" one, the stubborn, but also the more direct and tougher corporate managers. In many developments they did not follow Essen until years later, such as in the case of frozen foods and prior to that in refrigerated dairy products and fruit and vegetables. More creativity and flexibility in Essen, greater rigor and simplicity in Mülheim. Today's forecast would be likely to see Mülheim's ALDI South as the more successful organization in the future.

Discipline in retailing, especially in the discount business, is probably the most difficult of things to practice. Frequently the decision makers mistakenly assume that if 600 items work, then 610 will too, and probably 650. The problem is that this assumption in itself is not wrong. But where do you set the limit? It can only be drawn arbitrarily, and then it must be strictly enforced. But one thing is clear: every additional item certainly causes increased expenditure. What's more, the sales volumes of some similar product are frequently reduced and its significance in purchasing undermined. What's more, there are non-quantifiable influences on the organizational processes. ALDI does not draw up complicated calculations, but it did set rigorous boundaries for a long period of time. Within the established framework every employee could contribute his creativity and – like Einstein – grope his way toward improvements and better performance.

Basically, the widening of the product range at ALDI – more in North than in South – signals a change in values. In the organizational area, too, it can be seen that the delegation and control culture, which has been so important and successful at ALDI North, is changing for various reasons. The concepts are in transition. Especially the staffing of the highest executive positions in the administrative board has gone through such serious changes that there is no longer any assurance that ALDI North will be able to continue on course as rigorously and simply as it did itself in the past and as ALDI South still does today. The waning influence of the regional general managers will have a negative impact. The old, very motivating importance of each individual cannot retain its effectiveness in a group of 34 regional businesses and the administrative board. Growing – demotivating – central authority is the result. The administrative board could react to these developments with clever organizational changes. But, like any other company, ALDI will need boldness to carry this off.

The old guard of ALDI general managers in Germany, Friedhelm Bekes, Gerhard Bohnenstengel, Harald Schneidenbach, Peter Vianden or the first Dutch general managers Uli Schnier, Piet Conijn and Jos Simons, who were ALDIaners body and soul, have now retired. Alfred Bartosch, who had mastered the principle of ALDI purchasing like no other, has also left, as have the first members of the administrative board, Otto Hübner and myself.

But for all the question marks hovering over future theory and practice at ALDI, at present there remains the decisive ingredient, the enormous approval of consumers. That is a lead which would be difficult to throw away. The ALDI management now needs calm and composure in its competition with Lidl, Penny and Netto to be able to continue developing the ALDI concept.

In his 1997 bestseller, *The Dilbert Principle*, Scott Adams tells entrepreneurs that they will hardly ever find a management consultant who recommends that they keep everything the same. As a management consultant – one whose opinion has not been sought by ALDI – I would tell ALDI: "Keep to the successful principles and systems. Make changes only carefully and gradually. Focus on system maintenance instead of system change.

The explosive expansion of discounting competitors on the German and the European markets is putting ALDI under pressure. Short-term sales losses cannot be avoided. In 1997 and 1998 sales hardly rose in comparable geographical areas in comparison to the respective previous years. The same is still true for Germany in 2003. Such stagnation cannot be overcome by widening the product range, but only by the proven methods of uncompromising rigor and obsession with detail which are the sole ways of securing the competitive edge for the long haul. As

Metro's Erwin Conradi once accurately observed: the chances of a system's success grow when I know precisely which elements produce it – and these are the ones I must not touch.

Ingvar Kamprad formulated this idea for Ikea as follows: "We are a concept company. If we stick to the concept, we will never die." "Bare essentials," then, remain the basic challenge for the future of ALDI.

NOTES

1   Hans Otto Eglau, *Die Kasse muß stimmen*, Munich, 1972.
2   Astrid Paprotta and Regina Schneider, *ALDIdente – 30 Tage preiswert schlemmen. Ein Discounter wird erforscht*, Frankfurt a.M., 1996.
3   *Lebensmittel-Zeitung*, 2 July 1993.
4   *Handelsblatt*, 24 January 1995.
5   The administrative board of a private limited company in Germany may have supervisory as well as advisory and decision-making powers.
6   In 1961, Karl and Theo Albrecht divided their company into a Group South (under Karl Albrecht) and a Group North (under Theo Albrecht). Thereafter, the brothers conducted their operations separately in northern and southern Germany both financially and organizationally. Their headquarters were located near to each other in the Ruhr industrial area. Theo Albrecht was in Herten (later moving to Essen) and Karl Albrecht in Mülheim an der Ruhr.
7   Quoted directly from a lecture, *Lebensmittel-Zeitung*, 4 September 1975.
8   Hans-Otto Eglau, in *Die Zeit*, 3 July 1970.
9   *Lebensmittel-Zeitung*, 4 February 1983.
10 *Lebensmittelpraxis* 20/1992.
11 Nielsen, in *Capital* 4/1995.
12 Rolf Berth, *Erfolg. Überlegenheitsmanagement. 12 Mind-Profit-Strategien*, Munich, no year.
13 Dieter Wäscher, in *Blick durch die Wirtschaft*, 29 November 1996.
14 *Lebensmittel-Zeitung*, 12 November 1992.
15 Cuno Pümpin, *Management strategischer Erfolgspositionen*, Bern-Stuttgart, 1992.
16 Ingvar Kamprad and Bertil Torekull, *Das Geheimnis von Ikea*, Hamburg, 1998.
17 Peter F. Drucker, *Managing for Results* (Heinemann, New York 1964).
18 Ingvar Kamprad, op. cit.
19 *Blick durch die Wirtschaft*, 28 February 1997.

20 Donald K. Clifford and Richard E. Cavanagh, *The Winning Performance: How America's high-growth midsize companies succeed* (Bantam Dell, New York, 1985).

21 *Die Zeit*, 7 February 1997. Germans use the word "sauce" in this sense to mean a kind of uniform blanket cover that conceals and smothers everything.

22 Reinhard Höhn, "Die Flucht aus der Verantwortung," in *management heute*, May 1975.

23 *Wirtschaftswoche*, 9 September 1983.

24 *Lebensmittel-Zeitung*, 21 March 1997.

25 *Frankfurter Briefe für Unternehmensführung*, 23 November 1990.

26 *Blick durch die Wirtschaft*, 1 February 1995.

27 *Lebensmittel-Zeitung*, 6 December 1991.

28 *Lebensmittel-Zeitung*, 10 October 1997.

29 *Lebensmittel-Zeitung*, 10 February 1995.

30 cf. *Die Zeit*, 11 April 1997.

31 *Lebensmittel-Zeitung*, 11 November 1994.

32 *Lebensmittelpraxis*, 19/1991.

33 *Focus*, 18/1997.

34 *Lebensmittel-Zeitung*, 22 August 1997.

35 *Blick durch die Wirtschaft*, 17 April 1997.

36 Roger Fisher, William Ury and Bruce Patton, *Getting to Yes: Negotiating agreement without giving in*, (Penguin Putnam, New York, 1991).

37 Interested readers are recommended to read an essay in the *Lebensmittel-Zeitung* dated 7 March 1997 in which Roland Berger & Partner and the American The Partnering Group present the "European ideal model of category management" where they develop and illustrate the strategic ideas and measures with admirable charts.

38 *Lebensmittel-Zeitung*, 10 July 1992.

39 WISO-Tip, a regular broadcast on the second German national public television network, ZDF, shown on 15 September 1997, on the subject of supermarket cash registers.

40 *Lebensmittel-Zeitung*, 15 August 1997.

BIBLIOGRAPHY

Scott Adams, *The Dilbert Principle: A cubicle's eye view of bosses, meetings, management fads and other workplace afflictions* (Boxtree, 1997)

Karin Augenthaler and Paula B. Spielhof, *Aldi Piccoli. Das erste Aldi-Kinder-Kochbuch*, Zurich 1997.

Rolf Berth, *Erfolg. Überlegenheitsmanagement 12 Mind-Profit-Strategien*, Munich

Gerd Binnig, *Aus dem Nichts. Über die Kreativität von Natur und Mensch*, Munich 1997

Frederick P. Brooks, Jr., *The Mythical Man-Month: Essays on software engineering* (Addison-Wesley, 1984)

Donald K. Clifford and Richard E. Cavanagh, *The Winning Performance: How America's high-growth midsize companies succeed* (New York, 1985)

Klaus Doppler and Christoph Lauterburg, *Managing Corporate Change* (Springer-Verlag, 2001)

Peter F. Drucker, *Managing for Results* (Heinemann, 1964)

Hans Otto Eglau, *Die Kasse muß stimmen*, Munich 1972

Roger Fisher, William Ury and Bruce Patton, *Getting to Yes: Negotiating agreement without giving in* (Penguin Putnam, 1991)

Gesellschaft für Konsumforschung, *Aldi-Studien*, 1995

Daniel Goeudevert, *Wie ein Vogel im Aquarium. Aus dem Leben eines Managers*, Berlin 1996

Frank Görtz, *Der Einkaufsführer – Ein Ratgeber zum Geld sparen*, 1974

Gary Hamel and C. K. Prahalad, *Competing for the Future* (Harvard Business School Press, 1994)

Ingvar Kamprad and Bertil Torekull, *Das Geheimnis von Ikea*, Hamburg 1998

Niklas Luhmann, *Vertrauen. Ein Mechanismus der Reduktion sozialer Komplexität*, 3rd edition, Stuttgart 1989

Günter Ogger, *König Kunde. Angeschmiert und abserviert*, Munich 1996

Astrid Paprotta and Regina Schneider, *ALDIdente – 30 Tage preiswert schlemmen. Ein Discounter wird erforscht*, Frankfurt a. M. 1996

Tom Peters and Robert H. Waterman, Jr., *In Search of Excellence: Lessons from America's best-run companies* (Harper & Row, 1982)

Cuno Pümpin, *Management strategischer Erfolgspositionen*, Bern-Stuttgart, 1992

Eileen C. Shapiro, *Fad Surfing in the Boardroom: Reclaiming the courage to manage in the age of instant answers* (Perseus, 1995)

Shigeo Shingo, *A Study of the Toyota Production System: From and industrial engineering viewpoint* (Productivity Press, 1981)

Robert Townsend, *Further up the Organization* (Coronet, 1985)

James P. Womack, Daniel T. Jones and Daniel Roos, *The Machine that Changed the World* (Simon & Schuster, 1990)